...of daring temper

250 YEARS OF THE MARINE SOCIETY

RICHARD WOODMAN

Her Majesty The Queen
Patron of The Marine Society & Sea Cadets

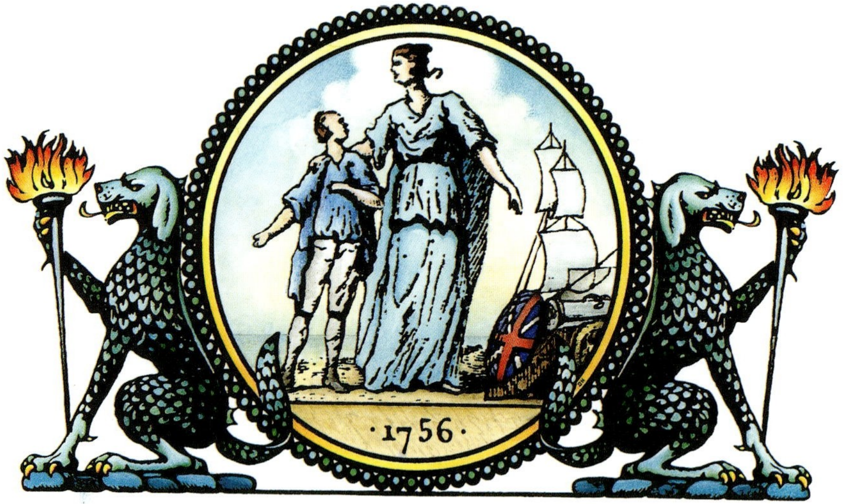
·1756·

CONTENTS

Hanway, vision and venture	1
Jonas Hanway encounters an enquirer	12
Officers and 'servants'	14
Vagabond boys	18
Recruiting the nation	22
The consequences of peace	29
Grand designs	34
Training ship *Beatty/Marine Society*	38
The Society and Nelson	41
A Marine Society boy at Trafalgar	46
Training ships *Thorn* and *Solebay*	48
Training ships *Venus* and *Iphigenia*	54
Schools, 'refuges' and 'reformatories'	58
Training ship *Warspite*	62
A Victorian sailor	64
Painful event and royal occasion	66
The seaman's lot improves	70
The voyages of the *Port Jackson*	72
World War I	76
Warspite III	81
Routines and rewards	84
Greater respect for seafarers	89
Studying at sea	92
World War II	95
New director, new directions	98
A *Warspite* boy 1936-1937	101
The torch of learning	102
Fifty pounds and off to sea	105
Under one roof	106
The winds of change	108
Metamorphoses and initiatives	112
Forward together	116
Officers of The Marine Society	118
Index	120
Acknowledgements	122

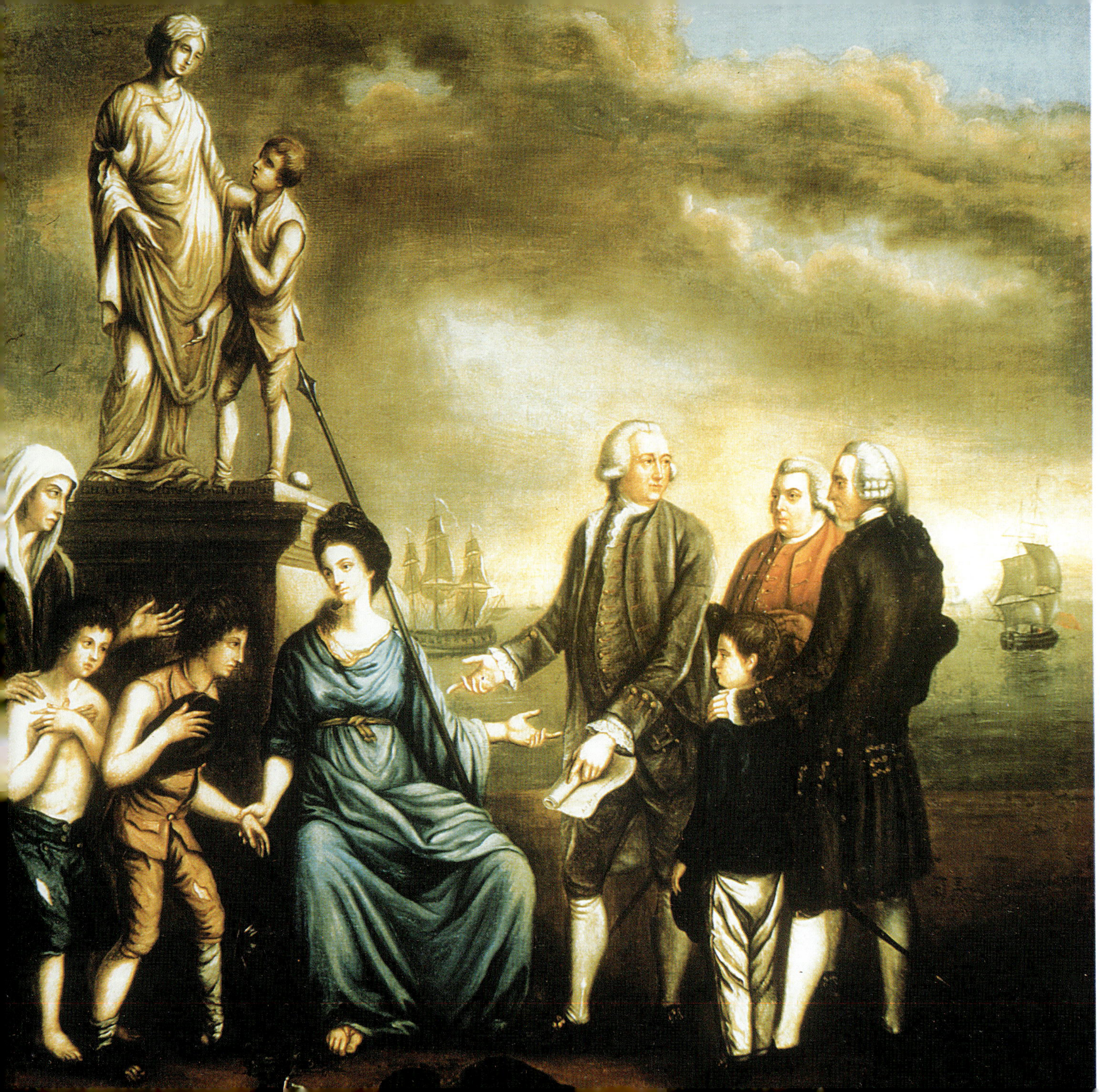

THE MARINE SOCIETY

ON the evening of 25 June 1756, some twenty-two well-dressed gentlemen, a few of whom wore swords, assembled at the King's Arms Tavern in Change Alley, Cornhill, London. Stolid, well-fed and self-confident, they had been called together by a remarkable individual who, like them, was of the mercantile fraternity. Known to educated men for his pamphleteering, Jonas Hanway was notorious among the City's riff-raff for his eccentric and habitual use of an umbrella, allegedly the first gentleman in London to carry one. Hanway's gaze regarded the world from a lined face that bore signs of an energetic interest in his surroundings and a character that would suffer neither folly nor turpitude in others. His presence conferred a sense of purpose on any meeting, and his eager quill was dedicated to expressing ideas which, for the greater good of mankind generally and Great Britain particularly, he felt needed articulation and implementation. It was out of concern for his country and its present plight that Hanway had summoned his friends, for Britain was at war with powerful enemies, and war was interrupting what Hanway and his fellow merchants believed the nation depended upon for its very existence: commerce.

Following several British attacks on French shipping and a series of hostile encounters between French and British colonists in North America, Britain was now at war with France. The Seven Years War began badly for Great Britain, but ended with her victorious. The spectacular defeat of the French in Canada by Wolfe and in India by Clive had been made possible only because of the domination of the sea by the Royal Navy and the exertions of the British mercantile marine. As Hanway and his colleagues gathered that warm night, success lay in the future. To the worried merchants it seemed that the war would irreparably damage trade, seriously weakening the nation and rendering it liable to defeat. As the conflict extended across the globe, British hopes of success demanded an unprecedented expansion of the Royal Navy. At the same time, the economic life of Britain, strained by the costs of the war,

An allegorical image of poor boys being transformed for the service of Britannia by the principal founding personalities of The Marine Society, Hanway, Romney and Thornton.

Edward Edwards.

placed equal demands upon her merchant ships' ability to carry imports and exports. One effect of this was to cause a shortage of competent seamen, the Royal Navy's traditional source being the very mercantile marine it had a duty to protect and which it plundered with cavalier disregard by means of the press-gang.

Alarmed by this, threatening as it did a large number of their trading firms, Hanway and his group of merchants and ship-owners decided to take the initiative and 'recruit the nation'. Motivated by patriotism, pragmatism and philanthropic virtue, they came up with the practical notion of encouraging men to volunteer and of sending to sea adolescent boys they had rescued from the indifferent streets of London, boys who were 'stout and well-made and have no disorders upon them further than the itch'. It was to this end that Hanway had convened the meeting that evening, and invited The Right Honourable Slingsby Bethel, then Lord Mayor of London, to take the chair. Unanimity and purpose soon imbued the gathering, as a consequence of which a new charitable institution called The Marine Society was established. John Thornton was elected its Treasurer and Jonas Hanway its Deputy Treasurer.

Hanway was to become The Marine Society's guiding genius. Born in 1712 the son of a naval victualling agent, and with a brother destined for a naval career, Hanway had become engaged in trade in 1729. He was first sent to Lisbon, where for twelve years he was involved in the flourishing Anglo-Portuguese trade in wine, fruit, cork and other commodities conducted through the 'English factory', the trading station of associated expatriate British merchant companies.

With Portugal under the arbitrary and absolutist rule of Dom João V, commerce in Lisbon was, in the words of the British envoy, Lord Tyrawley, 'done here with the utmost tediousness, difficulties and delays'. In 1739, when war with Spain disrupted traffic between London and Lisbon, it augured ill for Hanway's prospects. Under such difficulties, Hanway, now 27, learned patience and persistence, for war was to ensure his failure as a merchant but his success as a philanthropist. Even as his ledger columns failed to demonstrate profit, he also learned the importance of sea-power, in terms of both commercial shipping and a strong navy to protect it.

The indefatigable Jonas Hanway, busy with his pen, in his favourite chair which remains in the possession of the Society.

Edward Edwards, 1779.

He also came to admire Lisbon's charitable houses, some of which were dedicated to the needs of the chronically sick, particularly the leprous, while others catered for the orphans of both sexes teeming the streets of the Portuguese capital. But while Hanway enjoyed clothes of distinction, wore a sword to defend himself against the bold rapacity of footpads, and developed a penchant for what he called 'temperate wine drinking', he also imbibed the patriotism of the expatriate and a strong conviction of the virtues of mercantilism.

Hanway returned to London, invested his small capital and two years later, in 1743, became a junior partner in the Russia Company. During a long passage to Riga he gained 'melancholy impressions of the danger of sea life', being crippled by sea-sickness which 'nothing but the acutest distemper can exceed'. Travelling onwards overland he arrived in the Russian capital of St Petersburg on 10 June only to be dispatched forthwith by his superiors on a mission to determine the true state of affairs on the shores of the Caspian Sea. Hanway was soon embroiled in the politics of a frontier region. The Russians were pushing south and east; on the southern coast, Persia was under the ambitious heel of its self-proclaimed despot Nadir Shah, and the waters between the two were further muddied by English traders seeking to keep their enterprises afloat. Venturing into disputed territory, Hanway was caught up in a local rebellion and robbed. He and his party managed to escape but were compelled to flee along the southern shore of the Caspian in conditions of extreme privation. On one occasion 'The darkness of the night had been encreased [sic] by continual rain, whilst the wind, and the beating of the waves on the shore, together with the apprehensions of a savage enemy, added horror to the scene.' After twenty-three days, on fourteen of which he had been unable to remove his boots, and having covered 300 miles of rough terrain, Hanway reached safety. His subsequent adventures were to result, ten years later, in *An Historical Account of the British Trade over the Caspian Sea*, among the first of what was to become a prolific output of books and pamphlets from his quill.

On New Year's Day 1745 Hanway finally arrived back in St Petersburg, where his conduct was subjected to scrutiny by the factors in the English enclave and he became 'a martyr ... to the Persian trade'. Later he claimed that these tribulations exercised him 'in patience

The Baltic or East Sea, *c.*1743. As a junior partner in the Russia Company, Jonas Hanway embarked on the long passage to St Petersburg, a journey which prompted in him 'melancholy impressions of the danger of sea life'.

A correct CHART of the BALTICK or EAST SEA from ye Sound to Petersburg. From the latest and best Observations for Mr Tindal's Continuation of Mr Rapin's History.

EXPLANATION.
- Imperial CITIES.
- CITIES and Great Towns.
- Small Towns and Villages.
- Castles.

THE BALTICK OR EAST SEA

BAY OF BOTHNIA

PART OF SWEDEN

HELSINGA

NYLAND

FINLAND

GULF OF FINLAND

CARELI PART OF RUSSIA

UPLAND

SUDERLAND

PART OF SWEDEN

EAST GOTHLAND

SMALLAND

BLEKING

SCHONEN

EASTLAND

OSEL

GULF OF LIVONIA

LIVONIA

LETTENLAND

COURLAND

SAMOGITIA

INGRIA

PART OF POLAND

PRUSSIA

POMERANIA

BAHU HALLAND

Places labeled on map include: Niurunda, Hermangers, Hudwinkswald, Jettesholm, Eranger, Balsoon I., Agan I., Soderham, Prestorgrande, Hamrung, Jagar I., Uske I., Gevalie, Uevale, Dala R., Elsgasty, Formark, Oosthamar, Oregrund, Weddoe, No Talge, Aker, Ekro, Stockholm, Moller Lake, So. Talge, Teras, Nykoping, Norderkoping, Suyderkoping, Scheling, Sabuy, Westerwyck, I. Wrouenberg, Flyserly, Stickholm, Wen, Faro I., Farosound or Strait, Westergarn, Wisby, Oestergarde, Gottland, Narnwyck, Hornburg, Christiansloe, Ahuys, Calmar, Mokleby, Christianople, Bornholm I., Helsingsborg, Landskron, Lunden, Malmoe, Copenhagen, Roskild, Sleswig, Nested Fiord, Moen, Alholm, Walsterfjord, Rugen I., Wick, Agard, Wyck, Knegt, Jassenitz, Oder R., Camin, Cestin, Ceslin, Belt, Brusterorart, Lockere, Ruk, Koningsberg, Helgoland, Pawnesburg, Dantzick, Oliva, Elbing, Memel, Palangen, Hasigen, Lyba, Steenberg, Upsse I., Lybal, Sven Oort, Alenagen Castle, Windaw, Domberg, Cauveren, Keuverwyck, Dunemund, Peyfora R., Quernkam Cast., Salis or Lemsael, Runen, Domes Ner, Kyn, Anger, Lower Oort, Water, Jas Oort, Mano, Sergholm, Pernau, Vela R., Pots, Verder, Paters Oyster, Castle of Moen Sound, Hapsal, Dago I., Daijer Oort, Patros, Hondwyck, Honds Oort, Reeck, Wornis, Divoelgroend, Ossers Jen, Revel Bar, R. de Kock, Wranger, Hoogeland, L. Tichere, Rodersone, Ritzart I., Nova R., PETERSBURG, Crocinstat, Coporie, Calogna, Lavens, Feuerhoef, Biorko I., Lumalai, Rochel, Wiborg, Beckaming, Retusari, Perno, Ernosand, Borgo, Helsingfors, Kirkslet, Esbo, Helsing, Lueyn, Ingo, Rakborg, Ekenes, Meyko, Buero, Lohuuskerk, Werno, Kumila, Abo, Aland I., Nykyrk, Totsal, Kidas, Raumo, Nyrajoki, Ladahall, Biorneborg

PART OF RUSSIA

NARVA R., Juvagrod, High Land of Narva, Woesenburg, Tolsburg, Brecklom, Narva R., Ingria

The HARBOUR of PETERSBURG.
CARELIA
Ritzart I.
Croonstat
Croonslot C. The Road
Oranienbaum
Peterhof
Wasili Ostroow
PETERSBURG
INGRIA

R. W. Seale del. et sculp.

under trials … increasing my knowledge of the world'. Remaining in St Petersburg for five years, 'undistinguished in the crowd', enjoying 'the pleasures and business of life', recovering both his capital and his reputation, he became a senior partner in the factory. Hanway's encounter with the lawlessness of Nadir Shah's Persia was influential in forming his deep and abiding respect for the British system of government, of the value of the Christian religion and the union of church and state. Moreover, Hanway, who regarded merchants as 'the Honourable of the Earth', saw in the tension between the members of the English factory and the British diplomats in Russia, led by Tyrawley, who had followed Hanway from Lisbon to St Petersburg, a ridiculous conflict of interest based largely upon social pretension and without logical foundation. To accomplish what he regarded as a worthwhile objective, that of general social improvement, Hanway considered it was only necessary 'to relate foreign and imperial policy as closely as possible to the needs of British commerce' which in turn fostered 'all the pleasures of humanity' while simultaneously promoting 'national interest and honour'.

Hanway, now made independent by a legacy from an uncle, left Russia on 9 July 1750 bound for Danzig, from where he travelled overland by way of Berlin, Potsdam, Wittenburg, Dresden, Leipzig, Hanover, Hamburg, Bremen, Amsterdam, Haarlem, Leyden, The Hague, Delft and Rotterdam. Everywhere in these great commercial hubs he was in contact with the merchants who underwrote prosperity, especially those of the British factories. At the same time, he made enquiries into charitable institutions which, it seemed to him, were the only way of helping the poor and guaranteeing some evidence of Christian principles in any society. At the end of October 1750, he finally embarked on the Harwich packet and 'after a passage of twenty-two hours, the wind blowing hard from the east', he disembarked and took the coach for London.

Hanway's sojourn abroad had been more than a period of dangerous adventure, and he returned among his fellow members of the Russia Company in London with a mature world view. Fortunately, and perhaps providentially, he found himself among men who actively practised philanthropic self-interest. While it was widely recognised that some merchants

The Caspian Sea – the scene of Hanway's adventures in 1744 – according to the observations of Captain John Elton, author of *Elton's Quadrant* and Thomas Woodroofe, Master of the British ship *Empress of Russia*, who navigated the Caspian Sea for three years. Thomas Woodroofe presented the map to Jonas Hanway in 1745.

Vol. I. Front Chap. XX.
A Plain CHART of the CASPIAN-SEA,
According to the Observations of Capt. John Elton
Author of Elton's Quadrant,
& Thomas Woodroofe Master of the British Ship,
Empress of Russia,
Who Navigated this SEA three Years
Presented to Mr. Jonas Hanway of
St. Petersburgh in 1745.
by his most Obedient Servant,
Thomas Woodroofe.
SHIRVAN
LESGEES
MOGAN PLAINS
TALISH
PROVINCE OF GHILAN
PROVINCE OF MAZANDERAN
PROVINCE OF ASTRABAD
KHALMUCKS
ASTRACHAN
YAEIK
COSACKS
KARAKHULPACKS
DESERT
KORGAN DESERT
TURKUMANS
BALKHAN LAKE
Derbend
Kizlar
Shamakie
Baku
Astrabad
Reshd
Karragogaskoi Lake
The Antient Course of the R. Oxus
Marine Leagues 20 to a Degree
The Figures with f are Feet the other Fathoms.
N.B. This Chart mentions the frequented Places only, and such as are of Use to Navigators.
Publish'd according to Act of Parliament
J. Gibson sculp.
Longitude East from London

took an interest 'to save their Credit, others to retrieve it … others … do it Prudentially to increase their Trade and get [useful] Acquaintance', many such men were also aware that 'Pride and Vanity built more Hospitals than all the Virtues together'. The contemporary poet Alexander Pope commented that 'Virtue's ends from Vanity can raise' and noted that by this means 'God and Nature link'd the gen'ral frame, And bade Self-love and Social be the same.' Such a union of the pragmatic and the publicly beneficial seemed part of the Divine purpose. Known as 'Christian mercantilism', it was both spiritually and intellectually satisfying to men of Hanway's stamp.

Such men included the father and uncle of the great reformer William Wilberforce, Thomas Raikes, elder brother of Robert Raikes of the Sunday School movement, and John Thornton, who was to join Hanway at the foundation of The Marine Society. Indeed, so strong was the desire to engage in this robust form of Christian endeavour that a third of the Russia Company's Court of Assistants were to join the first General Committee of The Marine Society. After his return from Russia, Hanway had involved himself in a number of charitable institutions supported by the Company, to whose court he was elected. The Foundling Hospital for Orphans (founded in 1749) and the Magdalen Hospital for the rehabilitation of 'penitent prostitutes' (1758) were soon benefiting from his energetic administrative skills.

Events other than war had also conspired to prompt Hanway into calling his meeting that June evening in 1756. The previous year, Lisbon had been devastated by an earthquake, seriously affecting British commerce. But the catastrophe had also stimulated a generous relief movement in Britain to ameliorate the effect upon the local population, and stirred the principle of Christian charity among wealthy men of goodwill. Now the early progress of the new conflict with France was throwing into sharp relief what was perceived as a serious deficiency in Britain's ability to wage war, sustain overseas possessions and preserve her commerce. The critical factor seemed to Hanway to be a lack of manpower. Pitched against the awesome might of France, it seemed that, while few doubted British courage, Britain's human resources were inadequate to the task of defeating the old enemy. Moreover, the state-sanctioned but unsustainable abduction by the Royal Navy of trained able-seamen from the 'Merchants'

Service' seemed a self-inflicted wound that would prove mortal. It was in this atmosphere that Hanway developed his policy of 'recruiting the nation' and, in rescuing young men and boys from the horrors of vice and degradation on London's unforgiving streets, he foresaw the practical and beneficial potential of training them up for the sea-services.

Hanway himself was never a rich man. His donation of £50 made to the Foundling Hospital in April 1756 was the largest he ever made, but he gave tirelessly of his time, energy and talents to all the institutions with which he became involved. He had become deeply concerned with every detail of the Foundling Hospital, from campaigning for funds to establishing a proper diet for the children, ensuring the Hospital's drains were efficient and securing placements for the inmates as they matured. It was from considerations of the ultimate fates of the young men – the girls were usually placed in service – that the notion of fitting boys for a career at sea emerged. For this he needed money, and at the meeting at the King's Arms he was well supported. Thornton was already committed, but now Charles Dingley

A depiction of the great Lisbon earthquake of 1755.

Wood engraving from *'The subterranean world'*, London, 1887.

and John Cornwall backed him from the ranks of the Russia Company, while others such as William Wilberforce senior and George Peters, who had known Hanway in St Petersburg, mustered in support and brought with them members of the Society for Encouragement of Arts, Manufactories and Commerce, founded in 1754 and later known as the Royal Society of Arts, of which Hanway was himself an active member. Also among the twenty-two gentlemen were naval officers from the Impress Service who signalled the willingness of the Admiralty to co-operate and proposed the encouragement of adult volunteers, or Landmen. Once established in principle, and with Thornton raising subscriptions, The Marine Society thereafter held its meetings at the Merchant Seamen's Office in the Royal Exchange, where Hanway and Thornton took centre stage and began recruiting within a month of the Society's inception.

John Thornton was elected the Society's Treasurer and served until the end of the American War of Independence in 1783. His plain attire belies the fact that he was one of the richest men in Europe.
Thomas Gainsborough, c.1782.

The Foundling Hospital to which Hanway contributed.

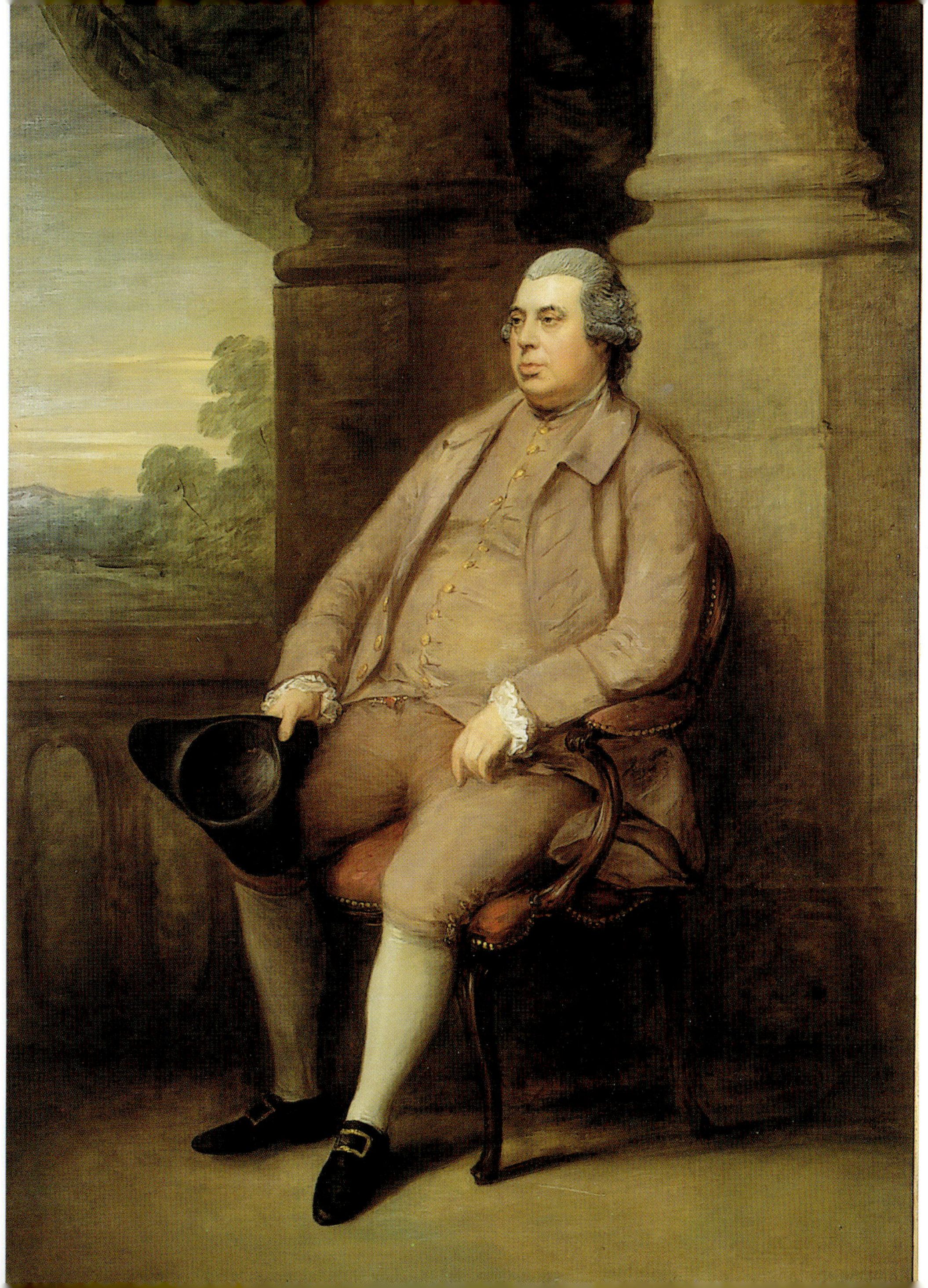

JONAS HANWAY ENCOUNTERS AN ENQUIRER

"You ask me if I am a philanthropist; well, yes Sir, I am, and no, I have no objection to the term. Though it may be a self-conceit I am, withal, unashamed of it.

If I may say so, Sir, philanthropy conveys two simple truths, namely, that if a man is fortunate enough to occupy a station in life which enables him to do good he must harness that vanity, which is natural in any man, to the public good. In this way one tames a natural vice and makes of it, if not a virtue, then something virtuous.

I am flattered – vanity again, I admit – you perceive in me more than the street urchins to whom I am known as a curiosity. On the one hand they know that I can fit them for the sea, but I fear they are somewhat intimidated by my appearance: the umbrella, you see. They find it so rare a contrivance that they laugh at me because of it. It is a sad thing, do you not think, that so useful an object as an umbrella can provoke mirth? It is a measure of their ignorance that they find it amusing, for the utility of the umbrella in both rain and strong sunshine is beyond contradiction. Yet, by conceiving it as a form of roof and by a contrary alliance of mistaken logic, they conclude a man who walks about London in the rain carrying a temporary roof above his head to be so ridiculous as to be risible.

'Tis wonderful, do you not think? Why, Sir, as you can see, it provokes laughter even in myself, though more from a contemplation of the pathetic want of the poor creatures, than from the carriage of my umbrella.

Patronising? Of course, but not maliciously so. You have only to review the work done by those Institutions in which I take an interest to determine that. Besides, without parents, who should patronise them but persons like myself? Witness the wretched condition of the Climbing Boys. Would you, Sir, see a son of yours forced up a chimney to labour within such filthy confinement? Of course not! Then why should Society at large, a body of people like ourselves, professing the Christian faith as a pillar of our State, countenance such employment? I shall tell you why, Sir, because it is convenient.

It is a very black irony, and I intend no pun, to see a boy sent up a chimney when a contrivance as useful as my umbrella could, with a little ingenuity be manufactured to procure a similar result. I have myself assayed a design of an horizontal broom made with a protracted and articulating handle which would render the sending of a boy redundant, but to what end? A boy is cheaper, and readily to hand, never mind that he may be abused and meet his Maker well before his time. The excuse is the urchin must have employment, or starve. What nonsense; there is employment enough at sea in his Majesty's Service or with the merchants' service.

So, Sir, you see how philanthropy may anger a man as much as any political dissension, eh? But set that aside. Utility, do you see, is something to be esteemed, as is plainness. Both are, perhaps, some way below Godliness and cleanliness, but surely all are the marks of a society which unites, or seeks to unite, its disparate parts. Utility may be applied to the umbrella as much as to that which seeks to serve the nation. Thus indulging vanity with a principle in the national favour conveys with it benefit to those whose fate would otherwise result in a descent into a vice worse than vanity. In this wise we may save the climbing boys and prepare others for service with the fleet, that being the chief purpose of The Marine Society.

My interest in such matters is natural, do you see. I was born with naval connections, within the spray of the sea the son of a naval agent and indeed, I have family intimately connected with the navy. I am also, among other public offices, a Commissioner of the Victualling Board, though do no more than many other well-intentioned men who seek the augmentation of our economy and a general benefit to our nation.

But I see I tire you. The dark corners of the human heart are like a swamp; no sane man ventures there for all is morass and danger. Mark me, though, I seek no monument beyond the institutions in whose founding I have played a small part. As for my vanity, which vice taints all men, I take pride in it. Enlightened self-love has its natural expression in social benevolence. Vanity builds hospitals, Sir, which is more than can be said for Virtue.

Mark me, Sir, Commerce is the link by which men are united. This is the mutual interest which ought to subsist between Christians, Jews, Mahommedans and Pagans; so long as commerce is conducted with integrity, it must produce a connection and harmony, such as constitutes an universal Commonwealth, among the whole race of mankind.

Now, Sir, if you will excuse me, I hear a clock strike and time presses. Good day to you. See it comes on to rain. Truly I advocate this umbrella... *Your servant, Sir.*

The Umbrella Man: Jonas Hanway, father of The Marine Society, was reputed to be the first man in London to make regular use of the umbrella.

Crucial to the success of the new Society was the skill of its Treasurer. John Thornton's family came from Kingston-upon-Hull, where his father had made a fortune and on whose death John came into a substantial legacy. As well as the sum of £100,000, he inherited a profitable partnership in soap and sugar 'manufactories' in Hull and the mercantile house of Thornton, Cornwall & Company in the City of London. Five years later Thornton married Lucy Watson, the daughter of his father's partner. John and his wife, both dissenting Christians, were active in the philanthropic movement and were attracted by Hanway's proposal to encourage volunteers for the navy with inducement beyond the Admiralty's cash bounty. The Society would provide physical rehabilitation, a suit of clothes, bedding, and a Bible for spiritual encouragement. In agreeing these measures Thornton and Hanway began a close working relationship that was to last until 1783.

They had been joined less than a year after that inaugural meeting by Robert Marsham, Second Baron of Romney. Descended through his mother from Admiral Sir Cloudesley Shovell, Marsham succeeded to the peerage at the age of 12 and was educated at Westminster, Eton and Oxford. He took his seat in the House of Lords at the same time that he became a Doctor of Civil Law and afterwards travelled to The Netherlands, studying French and Italian at Groningen. Preferring 'a mutton chop in my own house to all the fine things at the Great Men's Tables', he was said to be a man of 'great learning, elegant taste, and excellent judgement, and a hearty promoter of every useful and charitable institution'. Romney became central to the intellectual and charitable movements that – public hangings, the press-gang and debtors' prisons notwithstanding – made the mid-Georgian age so dynamic an engine of national change. Romney chaired The Marine Society's meeting on 17 March 1757 and when it was incorporated by Act of Parliament on 21 January 1772, he became President, serving in this capacity until his death in 1793.

Much had been achieved by then, though from small beginnings. The initial policy of the Society was to recruit both boys and landmen volunteers for the Royal Navy. Most boys entered the navy as 'servants', a classification less specific then than it now suggests, the liberal number of servants allowed on the establishment of a man-of-war permitting a wide

Robert, Second Baron of Romney, The Marine Society's first President.

Sir William Beechey, 1803.

interpretation such that officers' sons could be entered as servants in order to accrue nominal 'sea-time', even though most remained at home secured to their nurses' apron strings.

At the other end of the social scale many poor boys were entered in a ship's books as servants to the various messes of petty and warrant officers. In addition to fetching-and-carrying, blacking boots and generally ministering to their principals, these youngsters would be encouraged to acquire skills in seamanship. The nimble and intelligent among them thus had the opportunity to prosper and, 'bred to the sea' in this way, could rapidly rise in the internal hierarchy of the ship. Some literally ascended higher still, to become upper yardmen, adepts in the simian but serious art of sky-larking in the rigging, while a handful became warrant officers.

For each of his servants an officer received the pay of an ordinary seaman. He was not obliged to pass this on to a boy beyond keeping the lad in clothes and necessaries. The remainder supplemented his own salary and could act as an incentive to take an interest in the lad's welfare and progress. The captain of a frigate with a complement of 260 men was allowed eight servants, while the other commissioned and warrant officers were each allowed two. Even if a captain wished to retain one personal man-servant for himself and keep two or three places for his own or a patron's sons, there was still ample provision for poor boys. To encourage a stable crew and advance his own career, a wise captain took an interest not just in his own but in all the boy-servants because from these he could build what was known as 'a following' and more certainly recruit competent seamen in the future, rather than having to rely upon the Impress Service or his own financial resources.

All this is at variance with the popular image of 'rum, sodomy and the lash' as the prevailing management style of the mid-Georgian Royal Navy, and to some extent it represents an ideal rather than an actual system. The truth lay in between, with the regulations – or lack of them – permitting considerable latitude, while the reality of a serious short-fall of seamen on the outbreak of war drove captains to recruit wherever and howsoever they might. Conditions on board hardly helped to retain men; despite the penalties if caught, desertion was always a problem and often led to suspension of leave for the deserter's shipmates left

The Marine Society at work in 1757, using as premises the Merchant Seamen's Office in the Royal Exchange.

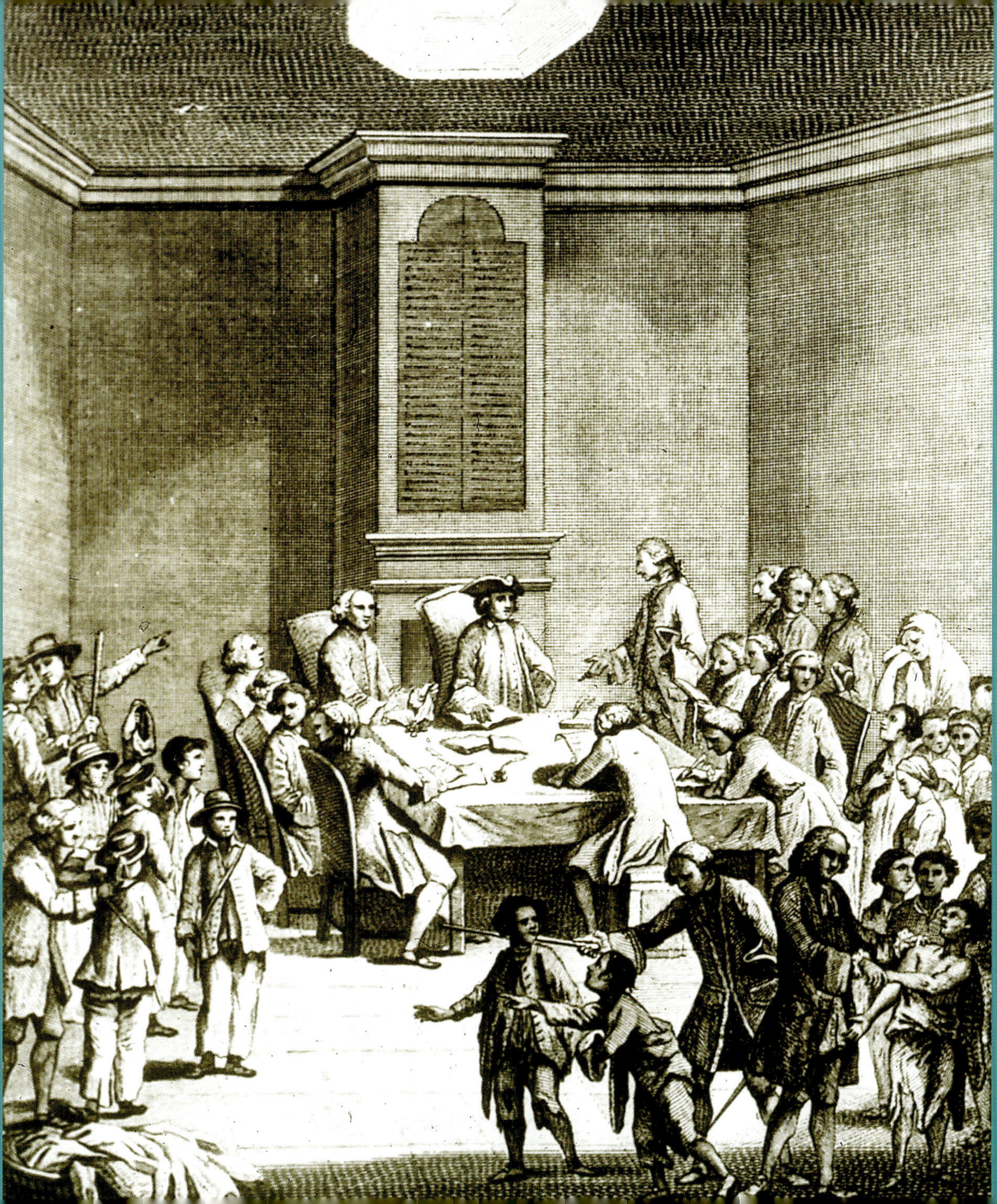

aboard, which in turn only exacerbated matters and created resentment. Moreover, there were other problems such as physical incapacity. Typhus was frequently brought aboard by insanitary recruits, scurvy arose from a poor diet and vitamin deficiency, and disabling accidents on board frequently causing serious ruptures together led to discharge and death rates that accounted for over nine-tenths of the navy's losses. Death from enemy action was, in comparison, minimal.

Into the Royal Navy's insatiable maw went the nation's seamen by the thousand, with an effect upon the mercantile marine that was immense and potentially catastrophic. It was to address this crisis that Hanway and his colleagues went to work. Hanway knew that although a bounty of thirty shillings – equal to the pay of an Ordinary Seaman and half that of Able Seamen – was given to landmen, malleable young recruits were of much more use. 'It is beyond all contradiction,' he wrote, 'that those bred to the sea ... generally become the ablest mariners ... inured to hardships they are not only rendered the more active and intrepid, but they can bear long voyages ... and change of climate.'

Hanway and his colleagues were not the only people sending street urchins to sea. The magistrate John Fielding did so regularly, basing his actions on a precedent established at the beginning of the century by a government desperate to rid the streets of vagabond boys. But Queen Anne's Act was flawed and, by the 1750s, largely ineffectual owing to the increasing urbanisation of the general population and a consequent rise in the number of the indigent. This produced a delinquent multitude to be hauled before the metropolitan justices by the score, and Fielding's enterprise was an attempt to find employment for these 'numberless miserable, deserted, ragged and iniquitous pilfering Boys ... shamefully infest[ing] the Streets of London'.

Fielding was the half-brother of Henry Fielding, also a justice of the peace but more renowned today for his satirical novel *Tom Jones*. Known as 'the blind magistrate', John Fielding was said by some to have been blind from birth, while others spoke of his having spent some time at sea as a young man, which suggests his blindness came later. Certainly he seems to have naval connections, and soon after the outbreak of the Seven Years War, his work in attempting the reclamation of wayward youths came to the notice of Captain Lord

Sir John Fielding, known as 'the blind magistrate'.
William Dickinson, after Matthew William Peters, 1778.

Powlett. Lord Powlett, afterwards Duke of Bolton, was short of men for his newly commissioned line-of-battle ship, HMS *Barfleur*. He contacted Fielding and provided funds for the clothing of thirty ragged delinquents, who were marched off to the 80-gun *Barfleur* lying at Spithead.

Word of Fielding's initiative spread, attracting the notice of others, not least a Mr Fowler Walker of Lincoln's Inn, who chanced to encounter the small marching column under its 'attendant' as it made its way down the Portsmouth road. Fired by the patriotic and philanthropic nature of Fielding's experiment, Walker began a subscription fund to clothe some three or four hundred such boys for the benefit of the Royal Navy. The idea gained momentum and attracted a small grant from the Admiralty along with contributions from a number of philanthropic gentlemen, including Jonas Hanway. Hanway's ever-active imagination was already entertaining similar ideas as an extension of his work with the Foundling Hospital, though less as a scheme for removing boys capable of felonious acts from London's streets than as extending help to the wretched urchins who lacked any prospects of earning a respectable livelihood ashore.

He was daily revolted by the condition of the clothing of the capital's poor and knew from his brother Thomas, then a post-captain in the Royal Navy, that 'The filthiness of landsmen's garments … occasioned distempers on our ships, which had proved fatal to thousands of men; and the filth and rags of boys could not be less pernicious.' The failure of the naval authorities to attend to this simple fundamental matter of welfare stands forever as a charge against them. Thousands of men perished through the lice-borne disease of typhus, then known indiscriminately as Ship, Gaol or Putrid Fever, which thrived on the over-crowded decks of a man-of-war and was a wanton squandering of precious manpower. That it took the private efforts of men like Hanway to put into practice what naval reformers like Dr James Lind had proposed some few years earlier was a scandal but, as the paucity of financial contributions from both the Admiralty and naval officers was to show, it was not then considered any business of either the naval authorities or its commissioned sea-officers to provide clothing for their men.

Individual captains, driven to distraction about manning their ships, began to perceive the benefits of this novel form of conscription but, as the navy expanded, not many had pockets as deep as Captain Lord Powlett's. A century later, the advantages of providing ratings with a uniform had become, with cleanliness and smartness, an obsession in naval orthodoxy, and while subsequent generations of sailors might bemoan the extremes to which 'bullshit' was to infuse their lives, it was the initiatives of far-sighted and dynamic reformers like John Fielding, Fowler Walker, Harry Powlett and Jonas Hanway, among others, that saved them from a stinking death.

Who exactly instigated the process of clothing landmen and boys for the Royal Navy is academic, though it was to be a source of irritation and occasional acrimony between Hanway and Fielding. Others, such as Charles Dingley, who had attended the inaugural meeting at the King's Arms, could also lay claim, and the probability is that the idea occurred simultaneously to several well-intentioned men and grew out of the earlier pragmatic, though failed, legislation of Queen Anne. Other institutions, such as The Foundling Hospital, The Stepney Society, The Royal Hospital School and Christ's Hospital, with its 'mathematickal boys' under the supervision of Trinity House, combined with a national inclination to send 'iniquitous pilfering boys' to sea in the merchant service, perceived seafaring as both a possible 'Destination to Navigation' if things went well, or a dumping ground if they did not. As Nelson's naval uncle Maurice Suckling phlegmatically remarked when he heard young Horace was to enter the Royal Navy, 'let him come and … a cannon ball may knock off his head and provide for him at once'. However many bodies wished to provide for sea-going youths, The Marine Society was distinguished by the scale, thoughtfulness and persistence of its efforts, characteristics due in great measure to Jonas Hanway.

Even as Hanway's new enterprise got under way, Fielding's faltered. By July 1756 the Bow Street magistrate had run out of funds and was compelled to apply to the newly established Marine Society for help. For some time the two worked in harmony but Hanway was always uneasy that the parties of boys forwarded to the fleet from the Society were, if not already criminals, then already identified as felons in embryo. Hanway sought to address the problem at source, to produce a grander scheme of proto-social engineering and, as history would show, to some extent he was successful. A man of lateral thought, he had pondered the effects of manpower shortages elsewhere in war-time along with the consequence of a peace, when demobilised and unwanted seamen were dumped ashore, fish out of water. Hanway wished to provide a genuine future for his recruits, whom he found among the 'distressed orphans, who wander about like forsaken dogs', the offspring 'of Porters, Chairmen and low Mechanics, [who] were obliged to steal for their Subsistence' and whose removal from the streets would benefit the boys individually and society generally. Most were illegitimate, others the children of migrant workers whose parents had died, or apprentices running from cruel or restrictive masters. By taking up society's debris, The Marine Society 'united charity and policy', watchwords which would ultimately be adopted as its motto. However, not all such vagabond youths were accepted; those of inadequate stature or who showed signs of ill-health, such as tubercular symptoms, were rejected.

A month after its founding, the Society appointed a professional secretary, John Stephens, and in due course more staff were engaged: a slopman to dispense clothing, a doorman and conductors to supervise the boys' marches to join ships. Initially, there was also a retained surgeon, John James, who checked the intake for signs of disease or physical weakness. Later, an apothecary named Henry Haskey undertook this duty, and an agent and reception premises at Portsmouth were acquired.

The founders formed an executive committee, usually chaired by Hanway as the Society's *de facto* director. It met weekly in order to properly regulate the Society's affairs, its management and fund-raising. Money was sought from and – with varying degrees of success – largely supplied by the founders and their friends, a disappointingly small handful of sympathetic naval officers, and other private subscribers such as David Garrick, who held two theatrical benefits for the Society. The King, upon whom Hanway and Thornton waited, also obliged. At the time, royal patronage was of immense and prestigious importance, not least in that George II donated £1,000 and the Prince of Wales £600. Lord Romney's cousin, Viscount Folkestone, and the Earl of Shaftesbury signed up in March 1757 and by May the

David Garrick, the actor and benefactor of The Marine Society.

Robert Edge Pine, *c*.1775.

committee consisted of fifty-two members, of whom twenty were drawn from the Russia Company and thirty-one from the Society for Encouragement of Arts, Manufactories and Commerce. Among the naval luminaries of the era who gave their support were Lord Anson, who had served as a reforming First Lord of the Admiralty; Earl Spencer, a future First Lord; the victor of Quiberon Bay, Admiral Lord Hawke; Admiral Sir George Pocock, the Master of Trinity House; and the victor of Louisburg and Lagos, Admiral Boscawen, who was to remark that 'No scheme for manning the navy within my knowledge has ever had the success of The Marine Society.' Other benefactors included Lord Clive, architect of British victory over the French in India, along with a succession of now obscure but active politicians, abolitionists and social reformers who inherited the mantle of those who first assembled at the King's Arms Tavern. Later, introduced by Romney, Nelson and his last flag-captain, Thomas Masterman Hardy, were also among the Society's supporters.

At the other end of the social spectrum, the resourceful Fielding, in his capacity as a magistrate, diverted fines from such sources as bakers 'feloniously selling bread of inferior quality' and penalties raised from reckless driving by hackney carriage-men. He also raised ten guineas from three gentlemen as 'Restitution for an Insult'. Subscription became popular among the gentry. Clubs as various as the Gentlemen of the Beef-Steake Society, The Society of Antigallicans, the Protestant Britons of Norwich and The Naval Club made donations, as did others from all over the country, particularly in centres of trade like Liverpool, where among ship-owners support for the navy and the protection it afforded to their trading vessels was of more importance than the removal of pilfering boys from the streets of London. In due course, donations arrived from the merchants of Calcutta and Bombay, and from Antigua, New York and Barbados. Hanway was an indefatigable lobbyist, letter writer and pamphleteer, failing only in persuading tight-fisted post-captains to open their purses more generously. The pool of skill and resource at its heart ensured that 'The Marine Society was from the start run very professionally, with a small number of paid staff and requiring very little fixed capital.'

Public relations were by no means absent from the Society's activities. Apart from pointing out the threat from the French as a powerful reason for its exertions, it claimed to have

The first Earl of Romney and The Marine Society's second President (1793-1811), resplendent in his peer's robes.

Sir William Beechey, 1803.

'cleared the land of 500 thieves', opportunistically omitting the qualifying adjective 'potential'. More spectacularly, the Society marked its first anniversary with a dinner and a parade of banner-carrying boys who marched to their own fife and drum band from the Royal Exchange to the Admiralty. Moreover, on the day of Garrick's benefit, *The Suspicious Husband*, seventy-five boys and forty landmen were drawn up on Constitution Hill by Fielding for presentation to King George II. His Majesty's countenance was reported to have been 'overspread' with 'a Smile expressive of paternal delight' as he slowly passed in his coach. After this mark of royal approbation, the boys marched off to the Admiralty, where Their Lordships appeared equally approving, after which the parade broke up in order to enjoy 'a Roast Beef and Plum Pudding' dinner.

However, it was at this time that a serious rift opened between Fielding and Hanway, provoked by the magistrate's inevitable selection of boys brought to trial for felony. Once in the navy, many turned out to be runaway apprentices and were followed by claims from their masters that impinged upon the emoluments paid to their new 'masters', the naval officers taking them up as 'servants'. This was too much, and in July 1757 The Marine Society denied direct entry into the navy from Fielding's office, a decision that caused the rupture between the two parties, and which by 1772 had led to the repudiation of Fielding's work.

The Society's original recruitment campaign was by advertisement. Notice was given to:

> all stout Lads and Boys who incline to go on board His Majesty's Ships, as servants, with a view to learn[ing] the *duty of a seaman*, and are, upon examination, approved by The Marine Society, shall be handsomely *clothed* and provided with *bedding*, and their charges borne down to the ports where His Majesty's Ships lye, with all proper encouragement.

And in order to lay a charitable ground-bait, the poster 'pasted up in the streets' added that 'if, in the meanwhile, any are in distress for want of the *necessaries of life*, the same shall be provided for them, in the most satisfactory manner at the Society's house, under the care of

Fireplace in The Marine Society Council Chamber, brought from its previous office in Bishopsgate.

Detail from the fireplace in The Marine Society Council Chamber, commissioned for the Society *c.*1780 out of Russian pine.

Mr Fluyd, in Grub-street.' More street urchins than might be supposed were able to read, and the poster concluded with instructions of how to proceed. Application was invited:

> to Mr John Stephens, Secretary to the Society, in Prince's Street, near the Bank; or to Mr John Franklin, accomptant and assistant-secretary, at the Society's accompting-house, in Bishopsgate-street, opposite the South sea-house [sic], on any day, from *nine* in the morning till *one*; or at The Marine Society's office, over the Royal Exchange, (where the clothes are given), every *Thursday morning*.

Although there were exceptions, such as the one-eyed Joseph Hall, boys had to be fit, 14 years of age and over four feet in height. Minor ailments were acceptable and Haskey cured the numerous cases of scabies revealed as the new entrants surrendered their clothes at the Society's office. After a thorough scrubbing, the boys were issued with a suit of clothes consisting of a blocked-felt hat, two worsted caps, a short blue or brown kersey-wool pea-jacket, a waistcoat, three shirts and three pairs of drawers, a pair of white canvas trousers, woollen hose, two handkerchiefs and two pairs of plain shoes. They also received a palliasse, pillow, blanket and coverlet, a knife, comb and sewing 'hussif' to keep their 'duds' in good order. Those items not worn were put in a seaman's canvas bag.

The extent to which the Society actually accommodated the applicants is unclear. Initially it seems that once medically examined, scrubbed and equipped the boys were marched off to Portsmouth or Chatham. Those who were otherwise suitable but temporarily incapacitated with easily curable skin diseases were put up until Haskey's ministrations proved successful. However, though probably for only a few days, boys with no abode were put under the supervision of Mr Fluyd in Grub Street. Here they were looked after at the Society's expense and given three meals a day, consisting of beef or mutton, small beer, bread, butter, cheese, porridge and broth. There are, however, indications that a curriculum of sorts existed too, even if it only included fife-playing, but this was given up in 1760 when there was insufficient money to retain the sergeant of footguards who had hitherto held the office of bandmaster. As it was next to Godliness, lectures in cleanliness were offered from early 1757 when the committee moved that it was Society policy 'to take care of their souls as well as their bodies'. Instruction in Christian morality, duty and the liberty of Britons was delivered by a schoolmaster, or dominie. Prior to leaving for their ships, the boys each received the Reverend Doctor Josiah Woodward's *Seaman's Monitor* bound together with a copy of Archbishop Edward Synge's elevating and patronising *Essay towards making the Knowledge of Religion easy to the Meanest Capacity*. The *Monitor* was not a manual of seamanship but a guide to morality and a sailor's behaviour when encountering foreign peoples, and the purpose of uniting the two volumes is clear. To add weight to the evangelical message, the boys also received a prayer book and a Bible provided by the Society for the Propagation of Christian Knowledge. Those recruits who were able to read were encouraged to help those who could not.

Hanway, Stephens and Franklin ensured that supply matched demand by regularly corresponding with naval officers to monitor the numbers of boys needed to fill their vacancies. Word of the Society's recruiting appears to have spread quickly and at least one boy turned up in 1759 to declare himself an orphan named John Chapman when he was in fact a runaway named Tom Brown. One effect of the Society's existence was to broaden the navy's recruiting base beyond the coastal regions, where seafaring was the traditional means of

The Royal Dockyard at Chatham. The first sight of the Royal Navy and the future for many a Marine Society boy.
Richard Paton, engraving, 1793.

TO THE King's most Excellent Majesty, This View of the Royal Dock Yard at Chatham,
Is by PERMISSION and with all Humility, Inscribed By His MAJESTY'S most dutiful Subject and Servant, Rich.d Paton

earning a living. In due course, the fleet's success at Trafalgar and the subsequent apotheosis of Nelson projected the appeal of the navy, initiating what became by the late-Victorian era a national love-affair with the genial and bewhiskered bluejacket.

The first draft of Marine Society boys left London in August 1756. Those destined for ships at Chatham or the Nore were at first marched to the Medway, but later joined the tender at the Tower. Those intended for Portsmouth always walked there, the march taking four days and the spectacle becoming one of the sights of London as they passed over Westminster Bridge. Some went on to Plymouth by ship. To increase the intake in 1757, a recruiting party was made up of three beribboned boys, two of whom were adepts on the fife and the third a former beneficiary who had spent some months at sea. In a touching demonstration of the Society's trust in them, the lads were given a small fund of three shillings and sixpence with which the party was to parade the streets and 'pick up all boys they can who are proper for the sea'.

Insofar as the fitting of landmen was concerned, they were given only a suit of clothes on application at the Society's office. They were also entitled to a small bounty, and it is interesting to note that one reason that the authorities refused to undertake the provision of basic amenities was that such largesse too often meant that the last glimpse the Royal Navy had of its new 'volunteers' was their disappearance into an alehouse. Presumably the landmen joined the boys in their marches to the naval ports, accompanied by their attendant conductors for, at the end of its first year of existence, the Society claimed to have 'fitted out 4,078 men and 2,797 boys to fight for their country'. A year later these numbers had doubled and by the end of the Seven Years War in 1763, drafts of boys were being sent from the shires, even from Edinburgh and from Dublin, where a sister Marine Society had been established. By this time the Society had temporarily suspended taking up landmen and was winding down its recruitment of lads, accepting only those utterly destitute boys sent there by magistrates.

Among those whom the Society clothed at its expense were boys appearing after naval officers had presented them to the Society's office for scrutiny and approval. Several unscrupulous gentlemen – assuming a philanthropist to be a fool in giving away his money

The Sailor's Return.

From an engraving by C. Mosley.

– tried to gull the Society into fitting-out their servants without formal presentation, and these were rejected. Sometimes this issue of clothing, when made to landmen, took place aboard the Impress tender at the Tower to prevent desertion. Many of the several thousand landmen joining the Royal Navy were therefore not directly recruited through the Society but entered under its aegis and so were eligible for the bounty paid only to volunteers. The wisdom of incarcerating these men in the same vessel as that used for holding impressed merchant seamen must be doubted, but that was the navy's problem, not the Society's, and in any case, the benefit attached to new men joining a ship with clean clothes, and thus minimising the risk of importing typhus, cannot be over-emphasised.

Recruitment proved to be a more complex business than at first anticipated, and much of Hanway's administration was bound up with discovering those whose entry into the King's service was compromised by unexpired indentures, felonious convictions and even previous desertion from the navy by those who returned to its shelter for personal reasons under assumed names. A few miscreants solicited clothes after county magistrates had sent them into the navy for punishment, an expedient course of action scarcely endearing them to the honest seamen among whom they eventually found themselves. But the notion that wild and aggressive behaviour could thus be converted to the benefit of the state was a kind of perverse extrapolation of the union between charity and policy that kept the Society's committee at its deliberations and Hanway at his desk. Nor was arrival at The Marine Society's premises always seen as beneficial; a few youths regarded it as a house of correction and escaped, mystifying the gentlemen philanthropists who would have given the youngsters their liberty had they but requested it. Such incidents produced a resolution that eventually resulted in a formal code of governance.

The victories of 1759 presaged the ending of the war in Britain's favour, and by 1762 the Society was considering its work done. However, the imperial expansion following the Treaty of Paris which formally ended the war in February 1763 opened up new opportunities for British trade, and Hanway continued his search for 'Boys of daring Temper whose genius leads them to try their fortunes at Sea', particularly those of 'too volatile a disposition for their trade, or [who were] too bold to live on Shore with sober Masters'. In fact, some people thought that many of the Society's boys derived little benefit from naval service. As objects of charity, they could be neglected or ignored by the officers to whom they were allocated as 'servants'; sometimes little interest was taken in their welfare, less in their education and none at all in their payment. It was publicly alleged that aboard a man-of-war, boys suffering such wanton neglect were driven together, to congregate in out-of-the-way places like the cable tier, and were contemptuously referred to by the sailors as ' 'Scape Gallowses'; all they learned was how to 'talk bawdy', chew tobacco and indulge in gaming, through lack of supervised work on board. No doubt this allegation was partially true, and it was certainly so in some men-of-war from which reports of ill-usage also emanated. However, with peace came the counter-view that a youth better learned his trade, and was better paid, if he shipped aboard a merchantman. Another problem also emerged, that posed by mass discharge of boys from the Royal Navy as it laid up most of the fleet. Neither Hanway nor Fielding wished for the streets of London to be flooded with young men disaffected by a sense of exploitation. The Society decided that as in due time hostilities would break out again, it should continue to exist for the general benefit of the nation and to be ready to meet any future manpower crisis. The committee also felt an immediate obligation to settle in gainful employment those of their beneficiaries who might return to them for help.

By happy chance, this aftercare was made possible by a revival in the Society's fortunes. In 1762, lack of money had put a stop to the issue of clothing to a dwindling number of boys passing through the Society's hands and was to defer recruiting for the time being. Nevertheless, the Society had recruited 10,625 boys and men, contributing some 5% of the total intake during the war. Now, Hanway had the pleasure of reporting that a William Hickes in distant Hamburg had died and bequeathed the Society a fortune of £22,000 provided that it continued its work. Unfortunately, a prolonged legal wrangle ensued. Hickes' family and some of his Hamburg colleagues contested the will and the Society had to appoint counsel to secure the bequest. Concern about the costs of the protracted case brought the Society's activities to a standstill for some weeks, until the summer of 1763 brought a second

A view of Portsmouth Harbour looking south-west to Gosport and the Royal Clarence Victualling Yard. It was here that, having marched from London, many Marine Society boys joined the men-of-war to which they had been assigned.

Dominic Serres the Elder, c.1770.

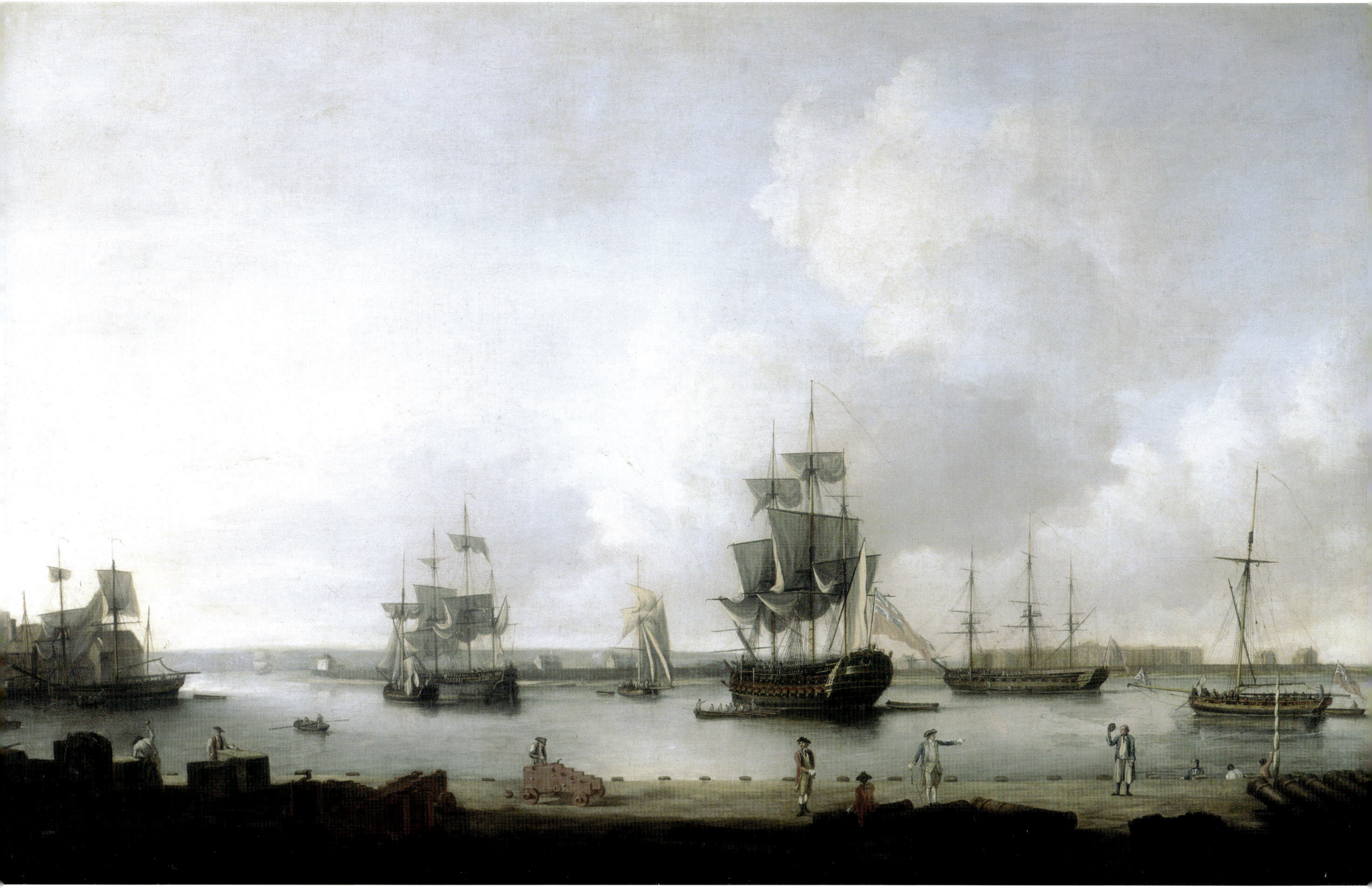

substantial legacy of £500 from a Richard, or Robert, Smith to swell the Society's assets. Furthermore, although attendance at meetings fell off, the level of subscriptions continued and much work devolved upon Hanway as he tussled with the consequences of peace. By 1763 most of the Society's beneficiaries had disappeared from the records, many having lost their lives in the general vicissitudes of the sea-service. Some had deserted, while others simply faded from an imperfect and idiosyncratic naval bureaucracy which regulated servants with some indifference. In fact, only 387 young men came forward for relief as the navy demobilised, and redundant men-of-war were placed at the Society's disposal as accommodation vessels at Chatham, Plymouth and Portsmouth, the better to deter discharged boys from returning to their old haunts. From these hulks those boys, numbering now only a few hundred, who were willing to volunteer were found apprenticeships with merchant shipping houses. The Society invited interested parties to apply to it and, using a standard indenture prepared by the industrious Hanway, many boys continued their seafaring careers.

Not all the boys were so tractable; Apothecary Haskey and a workhouse master at Hoxton, in east London, where some lads were lodged, complained of their insolence and intolerable behaviour. The Society attempted to resettle some boys ashore but potential masters all too frequently perceived the Society's role as a regulating body and its products tainted by criminal association. In many cases this perception was exacerbated by the likelihood of further corruption from their time in the Royal Navy, and unfortunately some associations with the Society ended unhappily.

Although it was July 1766 before Hanway reported to the committee that the Society had discharged its obligations in respect of post-war after-care, the committee had already debated its future purpose. Encouraged by the eventual prospect of securing the Hickes money, Hanway now produced a plan which argued the failure of earlier Parliamentary provision to secure adequate marine apprenticeships and mooted the idea that, since the nation would always want seamen, The Marine Society should make it its business to act as agent for the collection of poor boys and begin their metamorphosis into sailors. The Society saw as its plain duty the establishment of apprenticeships for boys who, through no fault of their own,

The Marine Society's original offices in Bishopsgate next to St Ethelburga's church.

were disqualified from the rudimentary parish relief provided under the out-of-date Poor Laws. Then, in early 1769, the Hickes bequest was settled and although only about half of the original bequest came to the Society, it was still an immense sum. At the same time, Fielding's own separate efforts in dealing with young felons encouraged Hanway to revive the Society's activities in the pursuance of apprenticeships.

One complication of the Hickes legacy was a requirement to assist girls. Between 1771 and 1778 some two thousand girls were found apprenticeships or sponsored in some way. This development prompted a move to incorporate The Marine Society, recognising its status and protecting its aims. Consequently, on 25 June 1772, an Act of Incorporation was procured, with King George III as Patron, initiating what became a line of royal patronage unbroken ever since. Also established was an almost, though not quite unbroken dynastic succession of presidents and treasurers. Successive Earls of Romney (they were elevated when Charles Marsham was created Earl in 1801) have served as president, and members of the Thornton family as treasurer. Two years later, in 1774, the Society slightly expanded its property at 54 Bishopsgate to accommodate its growing needs.

The shift from sponsoring boys as servants to preparing them for apprenticeships required a corresponding shift in the Society's thinking. Whilst not preparing boys for advancement beyond able seaman, the mercantile marine opened up opportunities for promotion to mate and master, the latter the rank of command of a merchant vessel. For this, a basic education was necessary beyond the moral encouragement, personal hygiene and 'the duties of oeconomy [sic]' offered by the original dominie. Now a schoolmaster was employed to impart the rudiments of English, mathematics, seamanship and scripture. This marked a radical change in The Marine Society's main objective: in the face of a worrying increase in the numbers of destitute and the rapacious in London, and the increase in rural poverty caused by the Enclosure Acts, the notion of providing more than the basic three R's of the Board and Dame Schools other than for the sons of gentlemen was quite new, but the benefit of the Society's continued existence beyond the end of the Seven Years War was soon to be demonstrated.

Civil disobedience in the thirteen British colonies in North America had quickly led to rebellion and the Declaration of Independence in 1776. What began as a local war rapidly escalated into a global conflict as France and Spain joined forces with the American rebels in revenge for Britain's earlier victories. It was to avail them little, though it secured the emergence of the United States as a sovereign nation. The Marine Society returned to its task of supplying landmen (or refitting distressed seamen) and boys for sea-service. Though many of the committee members may, like numerous liberal-minded and far-sighted British gentlemen, have been sympathetic to the colonial cause, the hostile posture of 'our insidious hereditary enemy', France, re-ignited the committee's enthusiasm as it increased the Royal Navy's burden. Among the intake of boys during the first three years of the new war were 94 vagabonds, 208 orphans found 'lurking about the streets', 509 sons of poor men with large families, 116 country boys, 40 Parish boys, 27 apprentices whom their masters wished to dismiss because of their incompetence or wayward conduct, 66 boys sent by the London magistrates as a reformatory act and a further 16 dispatched from country justices as being 'dangerous to the Community'. These involuntary entries were matched by a similar total of volunteers over the same period. Occasionally the youngsters distinguished themselves: two Marine Society boys wounded during a gallant action aboard HMS *Formidable* in 1778 were given monetary awards following a letter of commendation written by Hanway to Admiral Sir Hugh Palliser. By the time Great Britain finally recognised the independence of her former American colonies in 1783, the Society had in total raised over £85,000 and equipped 12,600 boys and 14,600 landmen for sea-service.

During the American War of Independence the Society's work had expanded further. In 1779 Hanway, Thornton, the Reverend Samuel Glasse (the first chaplain to the Society) and others had established a Maritime School in Paradise Row, Chelsea. This was intended principally for the orphaned sons of naval officers but it foundered in 1783, as the American War ended, for lack of subscriptions. Furthermore, the Naval Officers' Widows' Fund set up by the philanthropists in 1783 as part of their ancillary activities had been made possible by an anonymous donation of £10,000 in 3% Consols, or government stock. The fund

An illustration from the lavish prospectus for Hanway's proposed County Naval Free Schools, a grand concept which never came to pass.

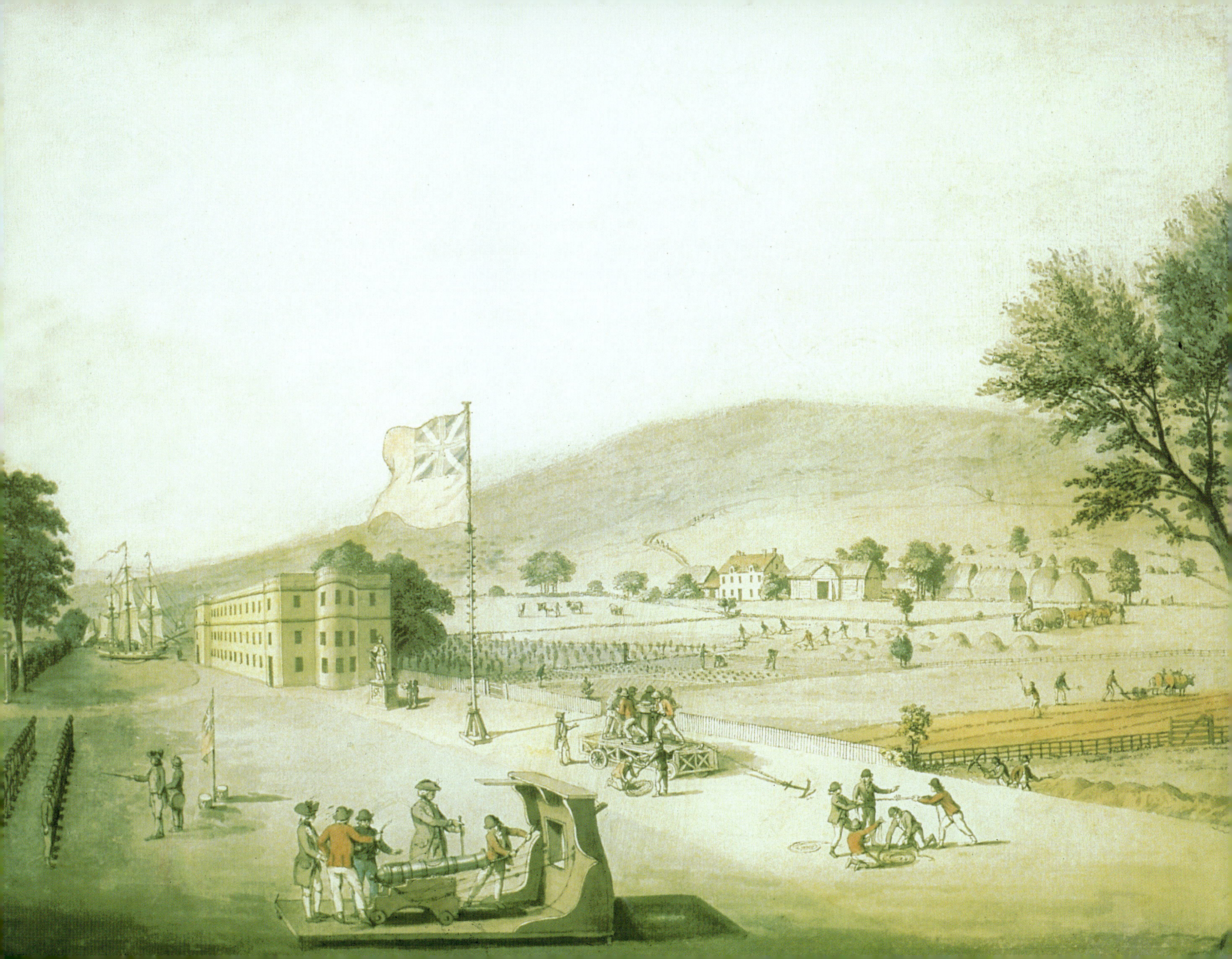

was to be held in trust and administered by The Marine Society, the income to be distributed to needy widows of commissioned naval officers. It was augmented in 1800 and again in 1809 by the proceeds of an appeal launched to erect a naval monument which never in fact materialised.

Undeterred by the failure of the Maritime School, Hanway returned faithfully to his original objective of saving poor boys, proposing in a lavish prospectus a national system of County Naval Free Schools. These were to be specially designed and constructed, with a hammock deck to replicate a ship. One hundred impoverished boys would learn seamanship on a large model ship within the school grounds and, to ensure each establishment was self-sufficient, would work on a 150-acre farm, raise crops and livestock for their own consumption, and an income from any surplus. This had the dual advantage in Hanway's eyes – and in defiance of the move off the land occasioned by the Enclosure Acts and the increasing mechanisation of agriculture – of providing alternative skills to boys who might not end up at sea. Even if this argument was flawed, Hanway's desire to provide the Royal Navy and mercantile marine with a steady pool of manpower drawn not from those on the brink of criminality but from an untainted background, was commendable, for he had long perceived the potential evil inherent in populating the lower deck with the dregs of society. His ultimate goal was not only to rid the streets of poor boys but also to rid the nation of the curse of the press-gang. Seamen, he concluded, being essential to the nation's wealth and welfare, ought not to have their personal freedom set aside in order that the majority of Britons could enjoy the liberties they were so fond of boasting of, as an infamous legal decision had ruled. Such a view was revolutionary; as late as the 1830s the novelist and post-captain Frederick Marryat incurred the displeasure of King William IV – himself a former naval officer known best for his tyranny – for proposing the abolition of the press-system.

After four years the ambitious idea had still found little favour, its sumptuous prospectus destined to become nothing more than an antiquarian curiosity, likely to excite only a few bibliophiles. A suspicion of such radicalism as Hanway proposed was, and perhaps remains endemic in British society, attached as it is to the necessity of raising large sums of money.

But Hanway's grand design was not entirely wasted. Just as his Maritime School at Chelsea closed, the Elder Brethren of the Trinity House of Kingston-upon-Hull – all merchant shipmasters and many of them commanders of Arctic whalers – opened a school influenced by, though not replicating, Hanway's elaborate proposal. They too clothed their boys, and the school exists to this day, the majority of its alumni having served at sea.

As Hanway's plan foundered, he too approached the end. He was brought to bed with 'a general infirmity of body' at his house in Red Lion Square on 5 September 1786. The 74-year-old man who, to the mirth of passers-by, had introduced the habit of carrying an umbrella on the streets of London, was laid to rest at Hanwell by its rector, Hanway's close friend Samuel Glasse. The interment was dignified by the presence of twenty-five Marine Society boys, all smartly dressed in new pea-jackets and trousers to march in the cortège bearing flags and ensigns.

Jonas Hanway had earned that mark of respect. He had never ceased to seek solutions to the social problems of his age, undeterred that these were immense and seemingly intractable; and while he might have come into conflict with the equally remarkable Fielding, he had held to his principle of uniting charity and policy with an energy and imaginative resource that astound us today. A tireless pamphleteer, Hanway promoted many Acts of Parliament, for the reform of prisons and workhouses, the creation of a metropolitan police force, the augmentation of public education, the advocacy of whole-meal wheat, the licensing and limitation of alcohol-selling premises, the promotion of inoculation against smallpox, and for improved sanitation, street paving and lighting. He campaigned for years to ameliorate the conditions of chimney-sweeping boys and for the reform of the Anglican church. In addition to his many charitable and philanthropic undertakings, between 1762 and 1783 Hanway had managed to acquit himself of the duty of a Commissioner of the Victualling Board, the body responsible for supplying the Royal Navy with adequate and edible provisions. While the commissioners had come in for their share of vilification, Hanway was as tireless and incorruptible in this public duty as in all his others.

Following Hanway's death, the old guard at The Marine Society gave way to the new.

John Thornton, in his 67th year, resigned as Treasurer, to be succeeded by his son Samuel, who was also a Member of Parliament. When he died in 1790, John Thornton was said to be the second richest man in Europe, with an estate of £600,000, then a fabulous sum, three quarters of which was passed on to his many charitable interests.

However generous the donations from Thornton and others, The Marine Society itself had had insufficient funds to build a prototype County Naval Free School, but the new generation of philanthropists was not hostile to the continuing responsibility of the Society to raise manpower for the sea-services. The idea of providing servants to men-of-war had long been abandoned and now, in addition to indenturing apprentices to merchant ship-owners, apprentices could be bound to naval warrant officers. These men were the technical experts of the day, appointed 'on warrant' to a specific man-of-war, unlike the commissioned officers, who could be transferred to another ship. According to its rate, every warship bore a number of these 'standing officers' including the sailing master, the surgeon, the purser, the gunner, the boatswain, the carpenter and the cook. Although the first few of these enjoyed sufficient social status to mess with the commissioned lieutenants, it was their technical skills that attracted apprentices or, as they were described on the muster-lists, 'mates'. The opportunity for an otherwise destitute youth to improve his station in life by acquiring the skills and ultimately perhaps the post of his master was a powerful inducement for the Society to embrace the idea. But learning book-keeping and mensuration, let alone navigation or the arcane mysteries of the pharmacopoeia, required a proper education under supervised conditions. To be complete, this education had to include the moral and Christian imperatives traditionally associated with the Society's policies, along with a basic knowledge of seamanship without which no man aboard a sailing vessel could comfortably exist.

With money in hand, Alderman Brook Watson proposed the acquisition of an elderly merchant ship on board of which boys would be properly and formally inducted into a life if not actually at sea, then at least afloat and subject to ship-board routine. Tenders were sought by advertisement, an annual budget of £1,800 was set, and in June 1786 the Society purchased for one thousand guineas an elderly merchantman, the *Beatty* of Liverpool, from

Hulks off the Royal Dockyard at Deptford, *c.*1840.

HULKS. DEPTFORD DOCKYARD AND STORE-SHIPS. ROYAL VICTUALLING OFFICE.

Messrs St Barbe & Green. St Barbe undertook to 'put her in proper repair and sell her hull, masts, yards, and two boats with such other stores as may be necessary for the purposes of the Society'. They would also 'fit the said ship with every accommodation for the boys computable to a plan laid before the Committee, and place her in such situation as shall be approved by the Society for a further sum not exceeding £300'. She was to fly a pendant, a jack with a red field and the cipher 'M.S.' and a red ensign with 'M.S.' and the legend 'Charity and Policy United' in the fly. The *Beatty* was moored off Deptford Creek, just upstream from Charles II's magnificent naval hospital at Greenwich. Watson and the committee having unimaginatively renamed her *Marine Society*, a tarpaulin bearing those words was stretched along her bulwarks for all to see. The first draft of her complement of one hundred trainees went aboard on the 13 September, eight days after some of them had attended Jonas Hanway's funeral.

The old man extended his benign hand from beyond the grave, for life on board was regulated by rules drafted by Hanway as his last act on behalf of the Society. The *Marine Society* was the world's first pre-sea training vessel and was run, as were all successive British static training ships, by a superintendent supported by a schoolmaster, who were each paid £5 per month. They also received a table-allowance of one shilling and two-pence, raised to two shillings in 1790, and each had a deputy: the superintendent a mate, the schoolmaster an assistant. Other staff included a boatswain and cook.

The trainees' rations were similar to those provided under the original scheme and, in addition to each boy's Bible, Book of Common Prayer and *Seaman's Monitor*, a dozen copies of Daniel Defoe's *Robinson Crusoe* were provided to ignite the enthusiasm of any boys yet to be fired with nautical ambition. The régime laid due emphasis on corporate and personal cleanliness; on theoretical and practical seamanship, including rope and boat-work; on the principles of navigation, and religious instruction. In preparation for naval service the boys were exercised at sail drill, 'fixing top and waist [anti-boarding] nettings', cutlass and gun drill. Even swimming seems to have been encouraged, despite the common sailor's popular prejudice against it. Sundays might be a day of rest but a parade, later known as 'Divisions', was followed by the ship's company transferring ashore by boat to attend matins at St Clement's church, Deptford. In the strong tides of the Thames, with the river often poppled by a fresh breeze, the boys would have become adept oarsmen and the best of them seasoned helmsmen, an asset to any merchantman or man-of-war.

In 1789 a curious little book appeared, purporting to be the life of one William Arnold, a poor boy who was rescued from penury and disgrace. It was almost certainly a tract, as the circumstances in the narrative are as improbable as the tone is moralistic. Arnold, hapless and cheated, fortuitously collapses upon the doorsteps of a house in Red Lion Square. Next morning the house-holder, Jonas Hanway, takes him to The Marine Society, where Arnold is out-fitted and found a place aboard ship. Here he is falsely accused by another Marine Society boy, an envious liar named Jack Hood. He and Arnold fight it out in the court of British pugilism, a scrap Arnold naturally wins. Elsewhere Arnold participates in a series of naval encounters which eventually bring him a commission and a respectable marriage. The book eulogises Hanway and philanthropy, and preaches the virtue of a strict education, especially for the poor, for whom the evils in urban life lay an especial trap.

War broke out again in 1793, this time with a France invigorated by revolutionary fervour. Except for a short break during the Peace of Amiens, the war was to last until 1815. The *Marine Society* was quickly bereft of boys, all having been immediately sent to sea. A subsequent scheme to train thirty boys for the merchant marine was not successful. Of 231 boys discharged over twenty-one months 'only 39 were apprenticed to the Merchant Service. Parish boys were advertised for, without fee, but the number of boys … dropped to zero' though not for long, as it was to The Marine Society that Captain Nelson turned for help when manning the 64-gun *Agamemnon*, the ship to which he had been posted at the beginning of hostilities. He wrote on 6 February 1793 asking Secretary John Newby for 'twenty lads' to be sent to Chatham, undertaking that 'the greatest care shall be taken of them'.

Before the month was out, seventeen boys were entered into *Agamemnon*'s books under the old system as 'captain's servants'. Four were 13 years old, the others a little older, including one of 18 named Thomas Bates, who had been a bricklayer but was illiterate. In fact, only six of the group could both read and write, though two others were able to read. Most importantly for the *Agamemnon*, they had all been schooled in 'knotting yarns … [and] exercising guns'. Nelson may have promised that they would be taken care of, but he did not scruple to flog four of them. One, 13-year-old Walter Holmes, for instance, received a dozen lashes for theft and in July 1794, when ashore fighting at the siege of Calvi in Corsica, he deserted. Two others, Richard Firbee and Charles Waters, were caught attempting to desert in October 1794 and both were severely flogged. Waters, rated by this time as an officer's servant, succeeded later in deserting at Genoa. Another lad, James Martin, received a condign punishment of thirty-six lashes on 10 May 1795 for an act with two Maltese seamen described as 'execrable'. The euphemism was deliberate and not coy, for in this way Nelson was able to spare Martin the death sentence imposed by the court-martial obligatory for capital charges such as sodomy. Whether or not the execrable act went that far is unimportant, but it shows the contemporary attitude, at least insofar as Nelson and the *Agamemnon* were concerned, as severe but practical. Martin was too useful a hand to send to the yard-arm on a whip, and in fact the following year he was promoted to ordinary seaman. He was one of ten of that draft of seventeen to have been promoted by the time the ship paid off at Chatham in the autumn of 1796. By then the rating of 'captain's servant' had been abolished, and the remaining four of the group were reclassified as 'Boys, Second Class'. Nor were any of them suffered to languish unemployed: over a dozen were immediately turned over to other men-of-war just then commissioning. Such was the trained sailors' lot in that epic era.

One boy in this generation achieved fame of another kind. It is unclear how Thomas Potter Cooke, born in 1786 the son of a surgeon, came to be processed by the Society, but he was in the navy at the age of 10, leaving in 1802 when the Peace of Amiens was signed. Perhaps he was a boy 'of daring temper', for two years later he went on the stage. In 1809 he was appointed stage-manager of the Surrey Theatre, where he was also to act until four years before his death in 1864. Around 1820 a print of him costumed as a gallant tar was popular and he was said to have been 'the best sailor … that ever trod the stage'.

Under Captain Nelson, the 64-gun *Agamemnon*, with Marine Society boys among her crew, cuts out a French corvette and gun brig in the Gulf of Genoa, 1795.
Nicholas Pocock, 1810.

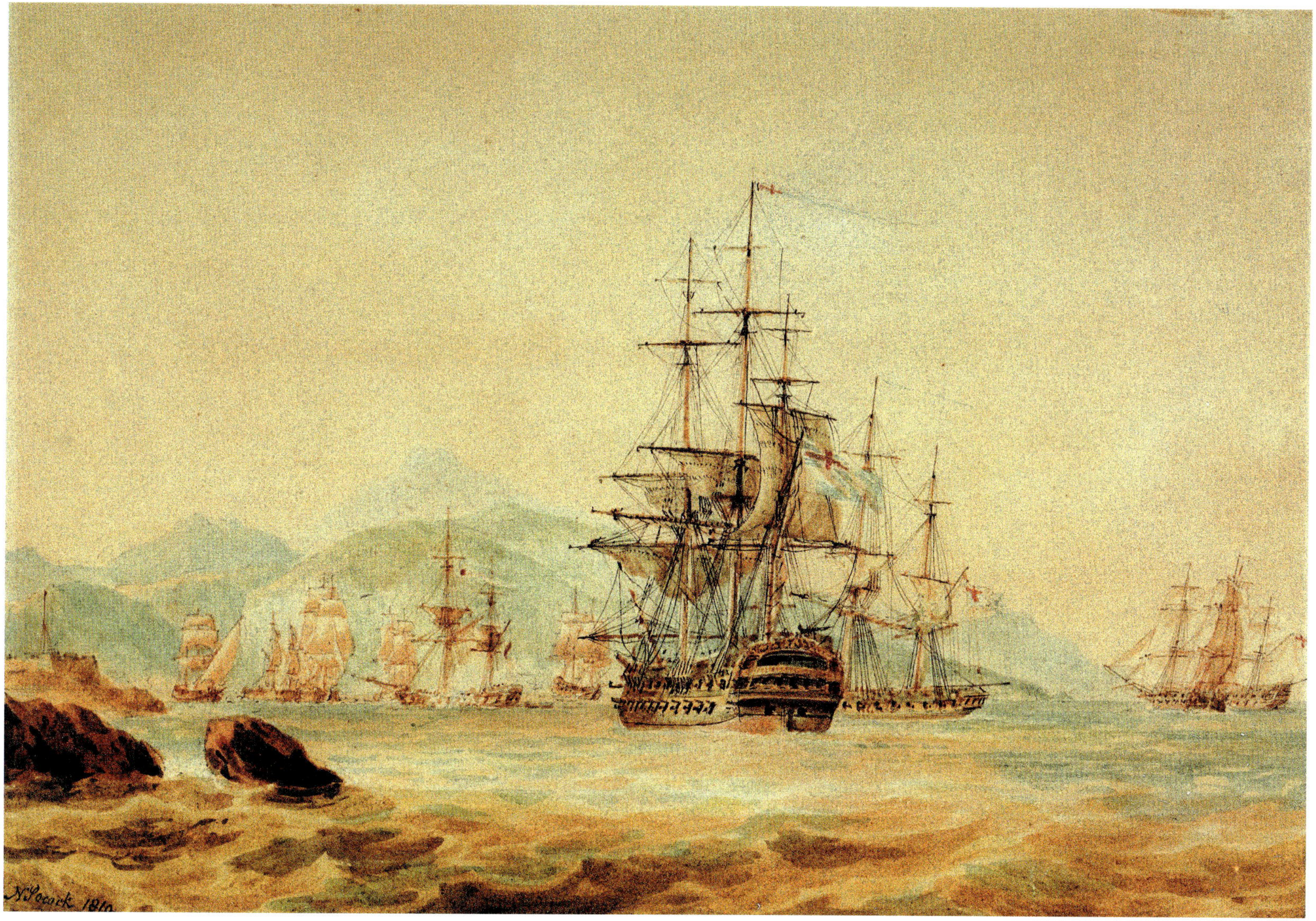
N Pocock 1810

The long and arduous war was to present the Society with its greatest challenge yet. By an odd and providential coincidence, the Society's finances had again received a boost from an unexpected quarter. An Act of Parliament of 1749 had set up The Westminster Fishmarket Trust to establish such a market on the south bank of the Thames. A subsidiary purpose of the trust was to apprentice boys to the fisheries, financed by a levy on all fishing boats passing inwards to the Thames past the Nore lightvessel. Whilst a considerable sum had been accrued, no fish-market had materialised and the scheme had lost momentum. In 1793 the assets were passed to The Marine Society, together with the accumulated levies less sixpence in every two shillings which went to HM Customs and Excise for their part in collecting the dues. The Society in turn sought to promote a Bill in Parliament to establish The Marine Society Fishing Company which was intended to train men and boys as a reserve for the Royal Navy. However, it was opposed by vested interests in the Commons and the Bill was defeated at its second reading in 1801. Nevertheless, the dues continued to be collected and paid to the Society until the original Act was repealed in 1849, overtaken by the Billingsgate Fishmarket Act of 1846. Although this contained a clause similar to the earlier 1793 amendment, transferring the lucrative dues to The Marine Society and, despite the subsequent existence of the Billingsgate Market for 135 years, 'not a penny was received by the Society from this provision of the 1846 Act'.

By 1799, a new concern was exercising the committee: the condition of their training-ship. The *Marine Society*, with a score of boys aboard, had been damaged by river ice and was making water. She was surveyed and condemned, news that alarmed the committee and, when they heard of it, the Admiralty, whose board recognised the value of a steady intake of boys and men from the Society. Although they had very few small cruisers laid up in ordinary, the Navy Board was instructed to make one available as a replacement. Initially the former bomb vessel *Racehorse*, part of the Phipps expedition to the Arctic in which the young Nelson had taken part, was put forward. With the berth empty, the Trinity Ballast Office dredged it out ready for the *Racehorse*, but in the end it was the *Thorn*, a small former ship-rigged 16-gun sloop-of-war which became the new training-ship.

A letter in Nelson's hand dated March 3rd, 1802, stating he was not fit to attend The Marine Society's meeting the following day, but sending a generous donation.

Merton March 3rd: 1802

Sir,
    As I am not well enough in health to attend the meeting of the Marine Society tomorrow, I have therefore to request that you will give the enclosed 5£ note for the benefit of the Charity and you will much oblige   Nelson & Bronte

Mr. John Newby
Secretary to the Marine Society_

A MARINE SOCIETY BOY AT TRAFALGAR

"Before I was took off the Streets by the Gennelmen of The Marine Society I was a climbing boy and treated Cruel by my Master. He came after me but soon Dissisted, the Gennelmen closing the Door against Him. I saw him soon afterwards, when he had found another Boy and knew me to be intended for the Navy. 'There are two ways out of a Chimney', he says, 'Either Up, or Down. But no Way out of a King's Ship but by Death', whereupon he gave a Grate Laugh and I saw him no more and Good Riddance.

When I was Taken aboard the Moored Ship belonging to The Society I was Washed and Cloathed so that my Mother, had she then Been Living, woud not have knowed Me. On board the Ship I was placed with other boys likewise situated and made to Thank GOD my Maker – and have done so every day since.

When we had conned our Bibles and knew the Knotts, Bends, Hitches and Splices, and how to serve a great Gun, we was Paraded for the March and with a Conductor proceeded to Portsmouth where I was entered into a Ship-of-War and in this Wise did come to join Lord Nelson' Fleet. I never did see His Lordship, but Heard much about Him and remember that upon October 21st, in the Forenoon, Much was spoken of him when the Lieutenant of Our Division on the Lower Gun Deck did repeat the Signal that Lord Nelson and England confided in us and that We shou'd stand to our Guns and Execute our Bounden Duty.

This we did with Fervour and dished up the Frenchies and the Spanish Mighty Well on that Glorious Day for Old England. Hearing afterwards of His Lordship's Death, I saw many an Old Mariner Spit and Curse most horribly, some even Crying like Babys that had been at the Cannon's Mouth all that Day of Battle. Our Lieutenant sayd that he was Mortified and that he had rather have Struck than have His Lordship taken from us, but afterwards our [Gun] Captain said that He was Overcome and Meant it Not. It wou'd have been a Terrible Disgrace to have Struck.

After the Battle there came on a Great Storm. Many Good Men were Drownded that had gone aboard the Prizes to Take them, for they were cast up on a Lee Shoar and Destroyed so that, for all our Trouble, we lost Much thereby and England's Glory was our Great Loss.

Men have been Saying that All this is the Common Fate of a Seaman but I say tis better than being a Climbing Boy. My name, sir? *Why, I'm Jack.*"

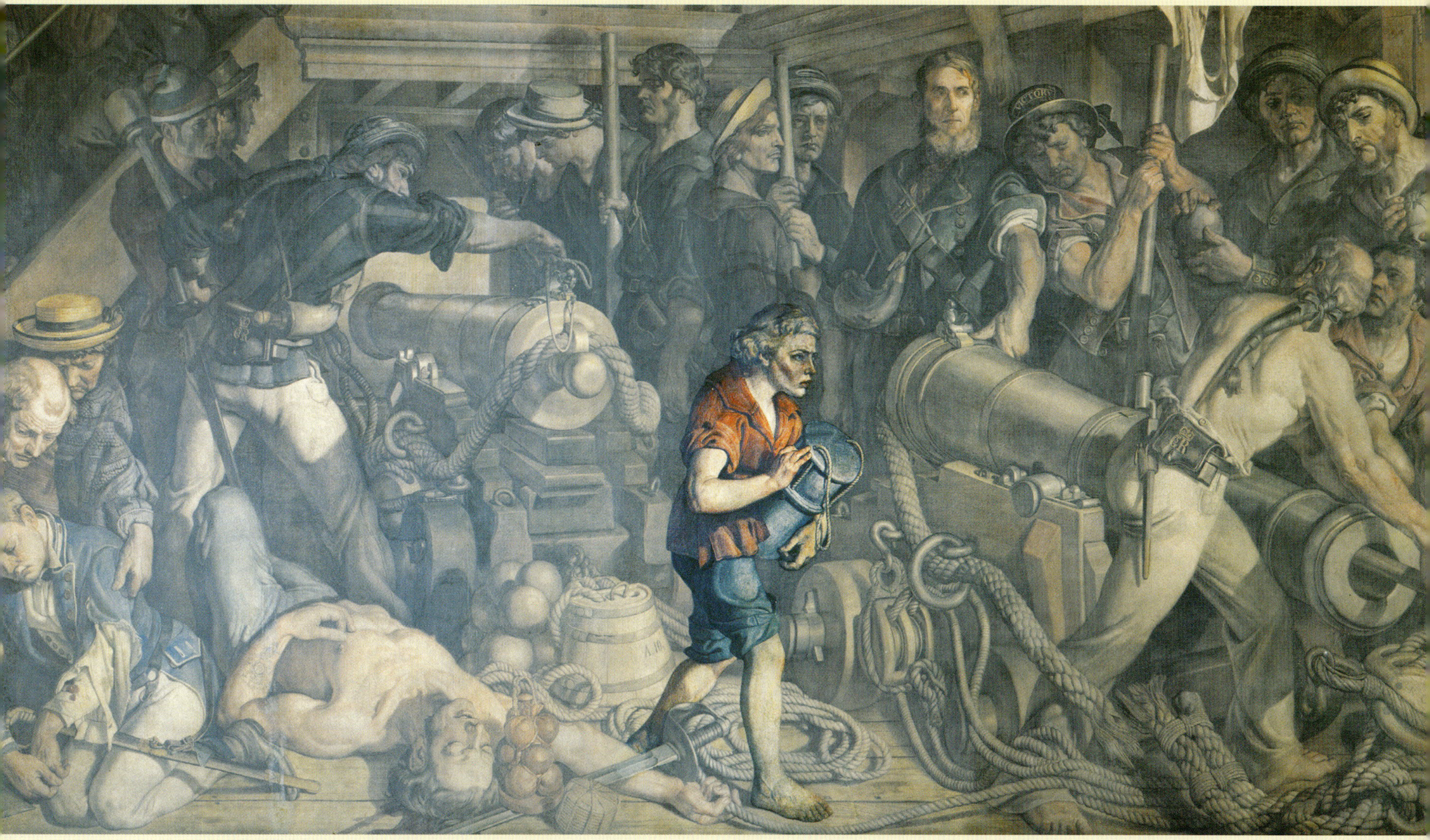

Shortly after her commissioning in 1779, HMS *Thorn* had been captured by two American frigates and passed into French hands. Retaken by the British frigate *Arethusa* after a few months under the Bourbon lilies, she returned to the Royal Navy until being laid up in 1783. Recommissioned, on 25 May 1795 the *Thorn* was in the West Indies where she fought a furious action with the 18-gun French corvette *Courier-National*. Commander Robert Otway's crew had repelled two attempts by the numerically superior French crew to board the *Thorn* and had, in the end, compelled the enemy vessel to strike her colours. Perhaps it was this adventurous past that dissuaded the Society's committee from renaming her as they had the *Beatty*. Perhaps the boys too were imbued with a sense of history being made and that, as they marched to Portsmouth or Chatham, their niche in it was assured, for this was the great age of the British sailor.

It was British sailors that made up the gun-crews and manoeuvred the Royal Navy's men-of-war, British sailors that kept their country's economy buoyant and able to pay for the war by manning her vast and obscure fleet of merchantmen. And it was to this mass of now largely unknown men that The Marine Society contributed with boys 'more confirmed in health, and more accustomed to habits of cleanliness', boys in whom duty and patriotism were inculcated by the frequent singing of *God Save the King*, *Hearts of Oak* and *Rule Britannia*. The output of the *Beatty* and the *Thorn* between 1786 and 1815, when the war ended with Napoleon's defeat at Waterloo, amounted in total to 14,485 boys and 24,739 men for the navy, with a further 3,754 entering the mercantile marine. When the war with France began in 1793 Britain's naval strength was 45,000 men following the partial mobilisation of the fleet in anticipation of a rift with Spain. Once a cold war with Spain became a hot war with France, the navy's appetite for men grew all but insatiable, rising to a high point in 1812, when Parliament voted the means to maintain a naval strength of 145,000 seamen and marines. In this context the Society's contribution was clearly significant and there can have been scarcely a single major fleet engagement or frigate action in which Marine Society boys did not take part. Indeed, such was the demand that in February 1805 it was necessary to order that no boy should be sent to sea until he had been 'at least thirty days on board the

A charming cartouche by C. C. P. Lawson showing a typical early eighteenth-century Marine Society boy '...of daring temper'.

Society's ship, that the Society's object may be the more attained of inculcating a sense of religious duties, of enforcing subordination of discipline, and qualifying the boys … in the line for which they are destined, to be more useful when sent from the care of the Society.'

By 1814 the *Thorn* was deemed to be worn out, her hull so riddled with gribble worm that she could no longer be relied upon to remain afloat. As a sloop-of-war she had not proved as satisfactory as the *Beatty*, since the boys slung their hammocks on the draughty gun-deck which, even with most of the gun-ports securely closed, must have been cold and spartan. The Admiralty again directed the Navy Board to find a replacement, an easier task now that the war was over, and accordingly the *Solebay* was made available. Built in 1783 as HMS *Iris* just as the American war ended, this former 32-gun frigate was larger and offered vastly better accommodation. Apart from her more capacious hull, she possessed below the gun-deck a berth-deck in which the boys messed and slept. Increased facilities for instruction were therefore available on her gun-deck, while cutlass drill and other exercises could be carried out on her upper decks where her boats were either slung in davits on the quarters or secured to booms extending into the tideway from the ship's side. The *Iris* was familiar on the waters of the Thames for she had been one of 'ten unemployed frigates' made over to Trinity House in 1803. This ancient Corporation had raised a large force known as the Royal Trinity House Volunteer Artillery whose task during the invasion scare then current was to man these frigates which were moored in the Lower Hope as a cordon of armed blockships obstructing the river. After the scare passed with the defeat of Villeneuve's fleet by Sir Robert Calder and then Nelson, the force was disbanded. The *Iris* then became a 'receiving ship' at Great Yarmouth, where she accommodated volunteers and men pressed from the fishing fleets until they could be taken by tender to Chatham and put on board active men-of-war. It was in this rather ignominious capacity that in late 1809 she took the name *Solebay*. Two years later she was moved south and hulked, that is reduced to a mastless accommodation vessel, probably lying in the Medway until partially re-rigged by order of the Navy Board in 1814 and taken up the Thames to replace the *Thorn*.

The *Solebay* remained in the charge of a superintendent, whose deputy was the schoolmaster. Under Standing Orders dated 21 April 1815 they were obliged to attend every day and sleep aboard on alternate nights and were answerable to the Society's committee by weekly report. Like the Articles of War aboard a warship, these orders were to be read aloud at Divisions once a month. A boatswain, carpenter, cook and boatswain's mate fulfilled the subordinate duties, looking to the well-being of the ship and her company. Spring and summer turn-to was at 0600, 'and at seven from Michaelmas to Lady-Day'. Hammocks were to be aired and stowed and the boys to wash, 'such of them whose state of health will admit of it, using the cold bath at proper seasons'. Prayers were said at 0800, when sick boys mustered before all hands breakfasted. 'School' followed until eleven, when sail drill, rigging or gun drill occupied them until dinner was piped at one. Seamanship, often in the boats under expert supervision, occupied the afternoon until four, after which the schoolmaster had charge of them for reading and religious instruction. Sunday forenoon was given over to Divine Service and Divisions, Monday to washing clothes and a full inspection by the superintendent and his staff. The petty officers, supported by a small number of senior boys, maintained ship's watches during the night, a gangway watch was kept at all hours and nobody could leave without permission. Visitors were discouraged, 'it being essential to the Society's design that as little interruption as possible be given to the discipline and oeconomy [sic] of the ship'. For the boys' health – ophthalmia seems to have been a problem from time to time – the *Solebay* was to be 'lime-whitened once a month'. By an Admiralty warrant of 2 October 1822, the *Solebay* was permitted to wear a warship's colours, including the Union Flag as a jack forward, and to fly a commissioning pendant from her mainmasthead consisting of a long blue weft bearing a St George's cross.

The *Solebay* was The Marine Society's training ship until 1833, a peaceful period but one of dynamic change in the maritime history of Great Britain. A ship which had been built for a forgotten war with rebellious colonists was to last through a period which encompassed the Industrial Revolution, the establishment of penal colonies in Australia, and the 'Great War' with France, the end of which confirmed Britain as the greatest sea-power in the world.

Lord Nelson, a Governor of The Marine Society.

Edward Bell, after Sir William Beechey, mezzotint, 1806.

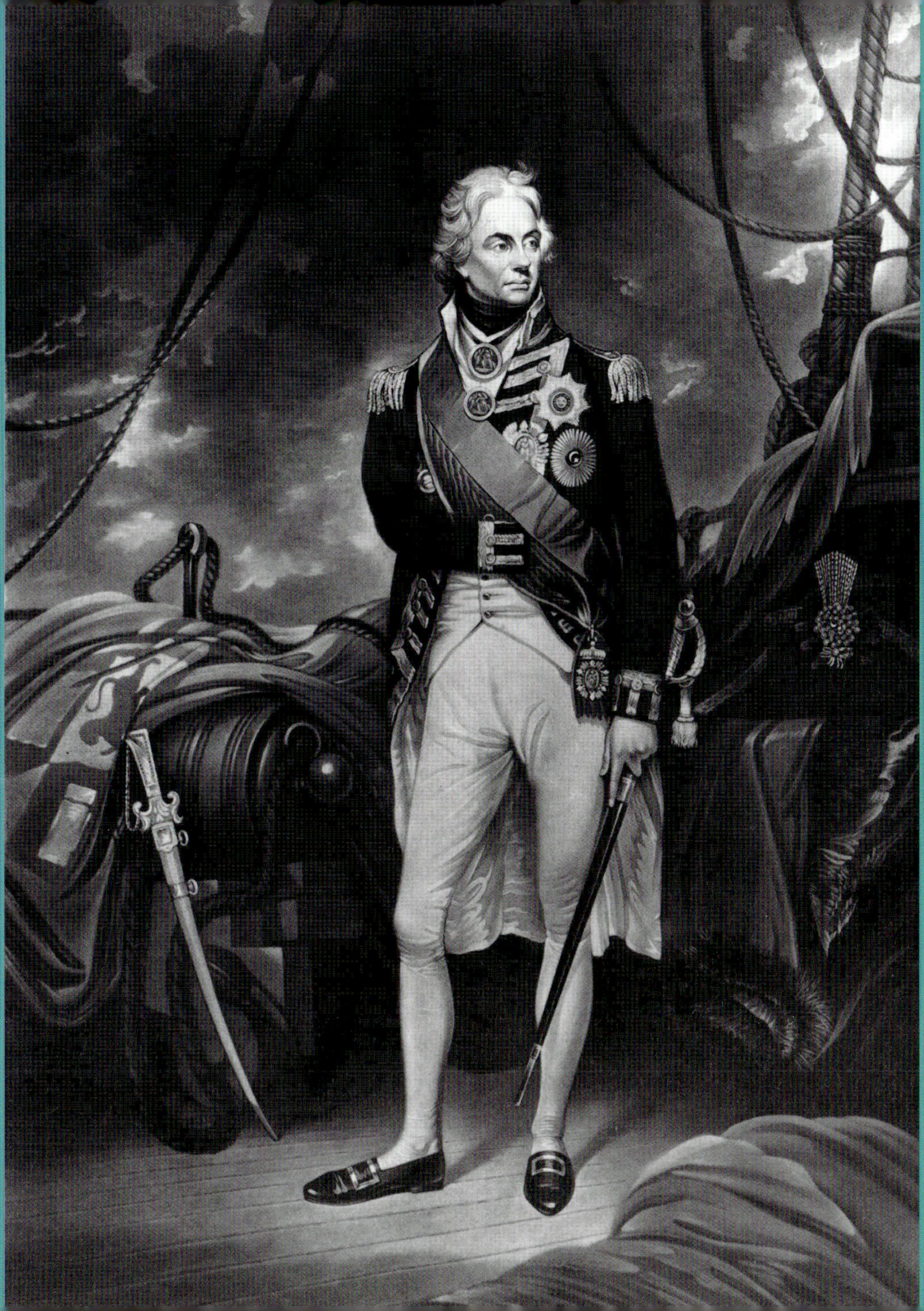

She was witness not only to the early paddle-steamers which first plied their trade in the service of coastal passengers, but also to a revolution in sailing-ship design which made possible a mass migration that followed the doleful export of convicts to the Antipodes.

The defeat of Napoleonic France brought peace but also brought years of economic depression, unprecedented unemployment and serious social disruption. Despite this, the commercial opportunities that the war opened to British and American merchant shipping were, in the long term, to be enormous. This was helped by a number of fundamental changes in British government policy such as the abolition of the old protective Navigation Laws by which the carriage of goods was restricted to British ships. This change encouraged free trade, as did a second abolition, that of the Honourable East India Company's monopoly of the direct carriage of cargoes between Great Britain, India and the Far East. Alterations made in the hull measurement used in assessing vessels for tonnage dues and Customs levies enabled new, faster hull forms to be developed, so that even while steam ships were appearing, sailing vessels enjoyed a new lease of life, one that was to ensure their commercial survival for over a century alongside power-driven ships.

All this was taking place as the Industrial Revolution was producing an increasing annual output of manufactured goods for which the world was eager in the growing numbers of British colonies and the wider world, particularly former Spanish and Portuguese colonies in South America. Such goods needed carriage, as did ambitious families who sought a new life away from the over-crowded and growing industrial towns of Britain. Parallel with increasing overseas trade went an expansion of the British merchant marine.

As far as The Marine Society was concerned, the immediate effect of the post-Waterloo depression was to terminate the recruitment of landmen. The ports of the kingdom were choked with desperate seafarers, many of whom were wounded, maimed and destitute, while others were simply unemployed. Paradoxically, merchant ship-owners anxious in difficult times to make a profit sought to man their vessels with an increasing number of apprentices who were a source of available and eager cheap labour. So although there was a diminishing demand for sea*men*, there was a corresponding increase in the demand for fit youngsters.

The ships of the East India Company were among the largest merchantmen in the world. They were armed for self-defence and had the appearance of men-of-war. In time of war they sailed to India and China in convoy, as seen here.

Nicholas Pocock, 1803.

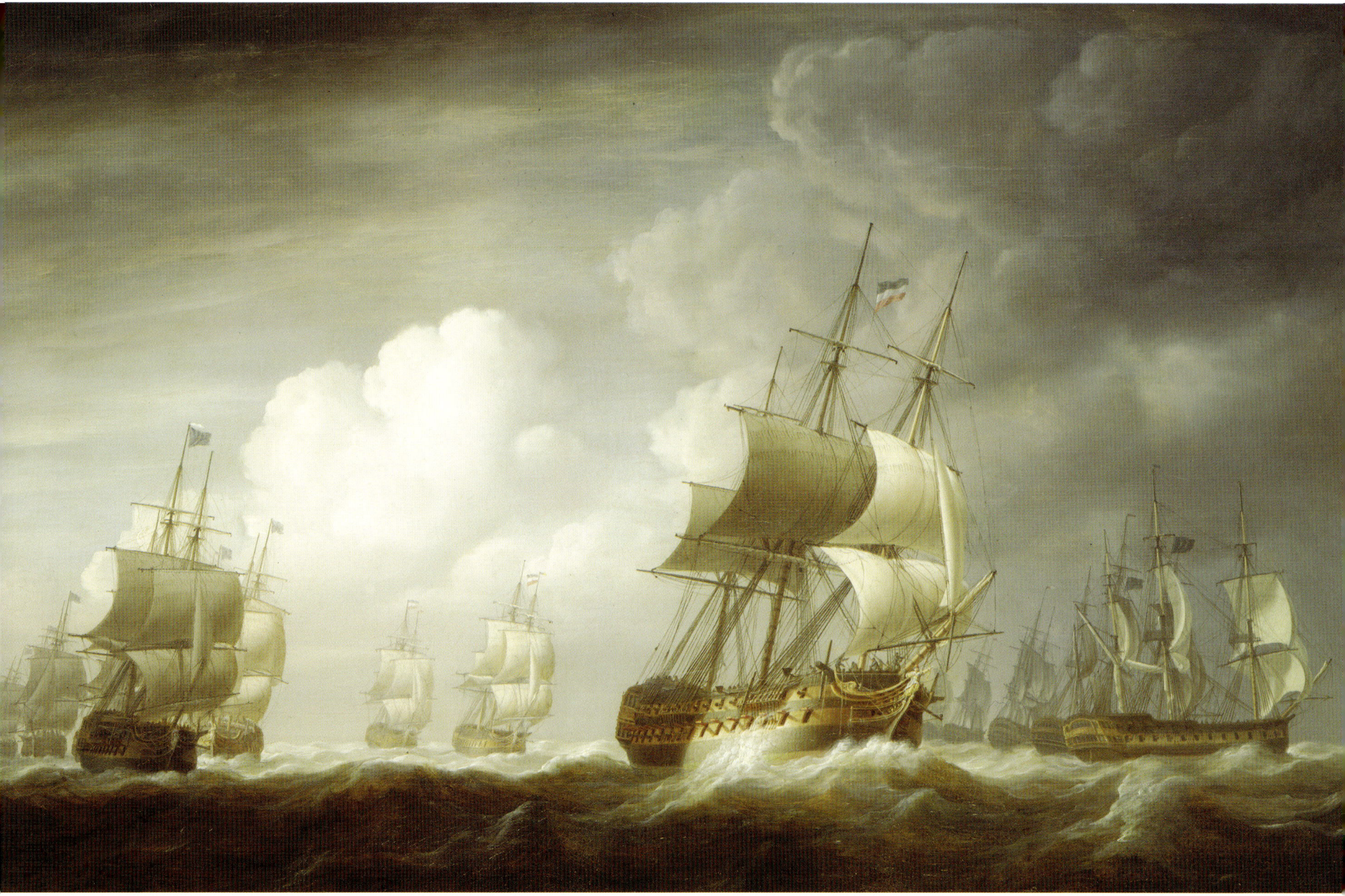

If they had already received instruction in basic seamanship, were adept at boatwork and inured to the routine of ship-board life, then so much the better.

During the half-century that *Solebay* and her successors *Iphigenia* and *Venus* were the Society's training ships, only 4,241 boys went into the Royal Navy, and although 3,760 were sent into the Bombay Marine, no fewer than 17,992 were sent to sea in merchantmen. With intakes of 100 to 120 boys, periods of training on board were ten to twelve weeks, a marked shift in both philosophy and policy on the Society's original limited objective of a few days during which a boy was issued with clothing and inducted into a basic appreciation of the Christian mysteries.

The *Iphigenia* was a 36-gun frigate built in Chatham in 1808 of 876 tons and with a gun-deck 137 feet long. She was to occupy The Marine Society mooring until she too was condemned in 1848, taken out of service and broken up in 1851. Her replacement was HMS *Venus*, which trained boys during a period of intense maritime activity, for not only did the demands of the Crimean War between 1854 and 1857 require an increase in naval recruitment, but the logistics of transporting troops, supplies and munitions to the Black Sea caused a shipping boom.

The *Venus* was a Leda-class frigate, one of the most numerous of all the Royal Navy's frigate classes, built in Deptford in 1820. Unlike the Bombay-built *Trincomalee*, which remains afloat in Hartlepool, she better resembled HMS *Unicorn*, which is also preserved, but at Dundee. The improved design of *Venus* and *Unicorn* incorporated a new form of stern, formally described as a 'circular stern', though more popularly called a 'lighthouse stern' from the form of the stern windows, which were embrasures properly angled to allow any guns stationed in them to traverse over a wide arc, and strengthened resistance of the frigate's hull against the tactic of raking. Not that the boys would have derived much benefit from this, the great cabin being the habitat of her captain-superintendent, invariably a pensioned naval officer. Like her durable sister-ships, *Venus* had seen little service but had been preserved and, like *Unicorn*, hulked. While *Trincomalee* underwent a refit prior to joining the British squadron in the Pacific Ocean and serving against Russian Tartary during the Crimean War, *Venus* was turned over to The Marine Society to take up a new mooring downstream off Charlton Pier, near Woolwich, a supposedly healthier location than Deptford.

The seaman's lot was being improved at this time by benefactions from charities whose governing bodies included members of The Marine Society's committee. The British Sailors' Society was founded in 1818, The Seamen's Hospital Society in 1821, The Destitute Sailors' Asylum in 1827 and The Sailors' Home Trust in 1829. In 1835 the Sailors' Home was situated in Dock Street with the Destitute Sailors' Asylum next door in Ensign Street. In 1843 evening classes in navigation were begun at the Home, by this time in receipt of royal patronage. The same year saw the setting up of the Wesleyan Seaman's Mission, later known as the Queen Victoria Seamen's Rest, and among the many other institutions which followed were the Missions to Seamen (1856), the Royal Alfred Seafarers' Society (1857) and, importantly, the RNLI. Numerous shipwrecks around the British coast had prompted the creation of local rescue organisations, and 'beach-companies' had been inaugurated in the closing years of the previous century. In 1824 these groups began to combine as the Royal National Lifeboat Institution, which, along with a newly formed Coastguard, encouraged the development of rescue apparatus such as the rocket-line and breeches buoy developed by Captain Manby of Great Yarmouth. Public awareness of the sailor's plight was increasing, owing in part to emigration familiarising ordinary people with shipping, but also to better communications and cheaper newspapers. One consequence was that public subscriptions to maritime relief became popular as the general wealth of the country grew and people had some disposable income. Revivals and reforms of Christianity went hand-in-hand with improved social conditions throughout the land, and society became more homogenised. The labours of the founders of The Marine Society were beginning to bear fruit on a national scale. Robert Raikes's Sunday Schools were by now an established feature of many industrial towns and had given birth to the Ragged Schools, while the Wilberforce family had done pioneering work in introducing in 1807 an Act abolishing slavery. In the following sixty years, the Royal Navy conducted an active and dangerous campaign against slave-ships of all nationalities. It may therefore be confidently supposed that in the first half of the nineteenth century the navy's small, fast sailing cruisers which chased and boarded the slavers numbered among their ships' companies young men who had first acquired their sea-legs aboard the *Solebay*, *Iphigenia* and *Venus*, and the ethos for which Hanway and Thornton had so tirelessly laboured made its contribution to the national psyche and the Pax Britannica. The new global spirit that increasingly imbued the British was a direct result of her steadily expanding maritime power, and behind this expansion of her merchant marine and Royal Navy, both even more dominated by steam ships, lay the quiet, steady work of The Marine Society.

Steam-power created another class of sailor, the stoker, or fireman as he was more likely to be called in a merchant ship. More and more young men went to sea than ever before, many excited in an increasingly literate age by the sea-stories of Frederick Marryat and others. Some measure of the power of Marryat's often interminable yarns may be judged from the fact that, in the years between Jane Austen and Charles Dickens, he was the most popular novelist in Great Britain. He and a handful of other writers established a genre that, despite our subsequent maritime contraction, is not yet quite dead.

These achievements were not without competition, for in the second quarter of the century Britain's merchant fleet had been under severe commercial pressure from that of the United States, but the outbreak of the American Civil War greatly reduced this rivalry, at least for a while. In 1865 the Sailors' Home was rebuilt to accommodate 500 beds, and the Mercantile Marine Offices were moved to their own site in Ensign Street. Nevertheless, all was not well within the British merchant fleet: the quality of British seamen was causing concern and was debated in a succession of Parliamentary Commissions, deliberations of Chambers of Commerce, ship-owners' trade associations and other such gatherings held intermittently between about 1830 and 1875 in an attempt to find reasons and remedies. Ship-masters had for some time lobbied for a means by which they might better regulate discipline on board ship, and government had become sufficiently involved by 1850 to pass the first Merchant Shipping Act and assume a measure of direct responsibility for merchant shipping.

The Marine Society boys at gun drill on board the first *Warspite* during the inspection of 1867.

The Illustrated London News.

GUN DRILL OF THE MARINE SOCIETY'S BOYS ON BOARD THE WARSPITE TRAINING-SHIP, AT WOOLWICH.—SEE PAGE 654.

Much has been made of the over-loading of ships and other abuses that led to the reforms of Samuel Plimsoll, finally sanctioned by Parliamentary Act in 1876, and the often rapacious capitalism of many ship-owners has been roundly condemned, but less attention has been given to the often poor quality of the British merchant seafarer in physique, moral character and skill. Institutions like the Sailors' Home and Red Ensign Club, which at the passing of the Merchant Shipping Act had also become the home of the Merchant Marine Office, had at heart the intention of improving the self-esteem of the individual seaman. Such organisations were powerless to improve his pay or conditions aboard ship – which were often appalling and remained so until the Second World War – but they could provide him with modest amenities away from the brothels and ale-houses to which he naturally gravitated, and where the whores and crimps of the great ports could batten upon his person until, stripped of his meagre pay-off from one voyage, they could ship him off drugged or doped on another. That he saw his situation as irredeemable made the seafarer an almost willing colluder in this precarious existence and, while a great deal of further legislation followed the 1850 Act, in which examination for certificates of competence were introduced as a responsibility of the Board of Trade on behalf of government, the rather more delicate matter of the men's calibre was left until 1875 when the results of an enquiry under Lord Brassey were made public.

The skills of the merchant and the naval seaman were no longer interchangeable as warships became technically more complicated, and the press-system was abandoned. The steam ship was acknowledged not to breed seamen of such consummate skills as the best able-seamen who excelled aloft in a sailing man-of-war. In due course, as warship technology required ratings to be specially trained, the skills of merchant seamen diminished in value to Their Lordships at the Admiralty. In 1858, Rear Admiral George Elliott told the Manning Commission that his

> experience with regard to merchant seamen had been enlarged from having been eighteen months captain of the port of Gibraltar, a magistrate on shore and on the water, and the shipping-master (on behalf of the Board of Trade). [Elliott considered

that] a man-of-war's man was as superior to a merchant sailor now in point of seamanship, as they used to consider, whether rightly or wrongly, a merchant sailor was to a man-of-war's man.

As Plimsoll emphasised the poor quality of many ships and the scandalous disregard by their owners for the safety and well-being of their crews, Brassey's evidence paralleled this with the unsurprising evidence that only those of inferior character, ability, sobriety and reliability could be found to man them. That the shipping industry felt less concerned with the issue is clear from the evidence of a 'most experienced and impartial witness', Captain Furnell, for twenty-one years the superintendent of a shipping office in London, who admitted that 'when in command himself he had had the greatest difficulties to get his men on board. He had gone down [the Thames] to Gravesend with few sober [men] on board.'

On the other hand, and perhaps more importantly, it was reported that 'The conduct of the British seaman in tempestuous weather at sea has rarely furnished cause of complaint to shipmasters and shipowners.' However, as Brassey – himself a wealthy yachtsman with a circumnavigation in his large yacht *Sunbeam* to his credit – puts it: 'I think it is true that the character of the British seaman, whether better or worse than formerly, is open to improvement.' By this he meant that the seaman's morals and his education were less than desirable and that efforts to improve them would be, and in many cases had already proved to be, beneficial.

By 1875 much was inevitably expected from the now considerable number of training ships producing boys for sea-service. When Brassey produced his report, the old *Venus* had gone the way of her predecessors and had been replaced by an altogether grander vessel. HMS *Warspite* was of similar vintage, having been built at Chatham in 1807 as a 74-gun Third Rate ship-of-the-line. She had been commanded by the Trafalgar veteran, Captain Henry Blackwood, during her first commission blockading Toulon, but her glory days had long since passed and she had been cut down, or razéed, to a Fourth Rate 50-gun frigate in 1840. In 1862 she was converted to a static hulk, turned over to The Marine Society and took up her moorings off Charlton.

At this time there were several such vessels: *HMS Conway* (founded in 1859) on the Mersey, and *HMS Worcester* (founded in 1862) on the Thames, were quasi-public schools for officer-cadets. Though not men-of-war they were dignified by incorporating the abbreviated form of 'Her Majesty's Ship' within their names, hence the full italics. Near the *HMS Conway* lay the *Indefatigable*, a training ship for ratings. Other ships were run as 'Industrial Schools': the *Cumberland* in the Gareloch, the *Formidable* at Bristol, *Gibraltar* at Belfast, *Havannah* at Cardiff, *Mars* at Dundee, *Southampton* at Hull and *Wellesley* on the Tyne. These, as another review of the British mercantile marine written by Captain Edward Blackmore in 1897 stated, were 'for boys not absolutely criminals, but who, if not cared for, might fall into crime'. There were also three so-called 'Reformatories' for under-age criminals, the *Akbar* and *Clarence* on the Mersey, and the *Cornwall* at Purfleet on the Thames. Both the Industrial Schools and the Reformatories were 'supported wholly or in part by the authorities (i.e. the state)'. So too were the 'Refuges' *Chichester* and *Arethusa*, which lay near the *Warspite* off Woolwich, and were run by the Shaftesbury Society for the care of orphans, while another ratings' training-ship, *Goliath*, lay at Grays.

Blackmore was principally interested in the training of potential officers. He deplored the failure of the Marine Department of the Board of Trade to make the education of seafarers a matter of national, that is to say governmental, responsibility twenty years *after* Brassey's report. 'None of these training ships can be esteemed as fitted for the training of young officers,' Brassey concluded, excluding *Worcester* and *Conway*,

> although … a fair education is given, and to some, the elements of navigation are offered; and those boys, who are fortunate enough to be apprenticed from the [training] ships to good [ship-] owners, have a chance to succeed, by good conduct, in rising in the service. But as seminaries for seamen they serve a useful purpose, although even in that direction their efforts are limited, the average number sent to sea from them being only about 1,400 per annum, of whom a goodly number go as cooks and stewards, and not as sailors.

The first *Warspite* on active service. Built as a 74-gun line of battleship in 1807, she was razéed to a 50-gun frigate in 1840.

The Society's first *Warspite* as a training ship.

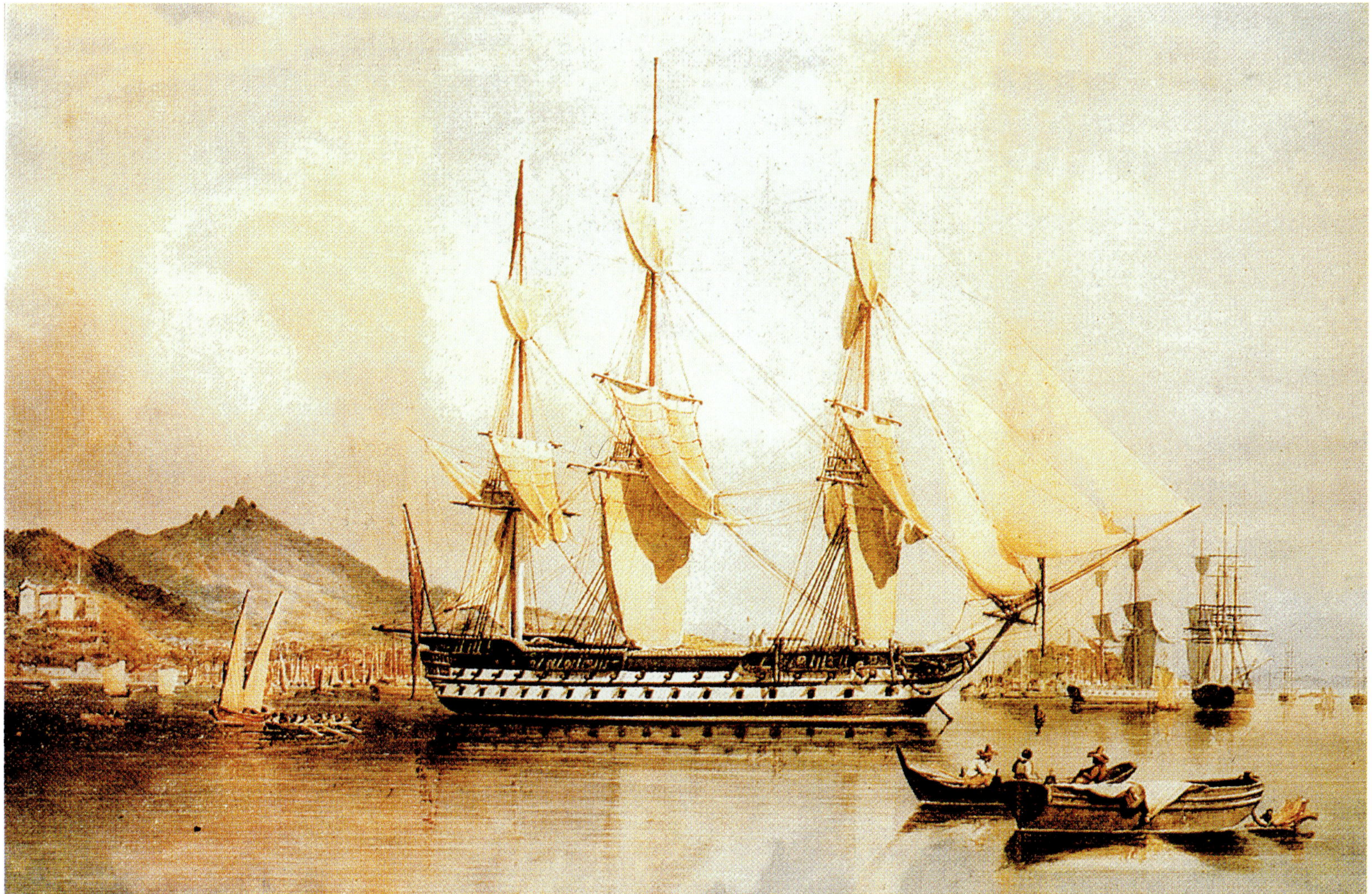

This was rather grudging praise and, of course, not all sent boys to sea, the Reformatories in particular being places of correction, not training ships. There was, besides, a resistance to the wholesale import of boys of dubious origin and ambiguous character into the mercantile marine. The double-edged expedience of, on the one hand, ridding mainstream society of potential nuisances, and on the other filling berths at a low wage-rate, was opposed by the more altruistic social engineers of the day. Brassey had earlier declared that

> Desirable as it is to make an effort to reclaim the unfortunate children of the pauper or criminal classes, it must be admitted that, in introducing boys of this class in large numbers into the merchant service, we incur a serious risk. The calling of the seaman must inevitably be lowered in the estimation of the honest and independent working population, if we allow it to become a general and recognised refuge for the destitute.

Brassey had gone on to say that 'it is a grave error to suppose that the dregs of society can be educated for a sea life,' adding the critical factor: 'A sailor, to be worth anything, must be physically strong and healthy.' He concluded rather sanctimoniously that 'we must begin by attracting boys to the sea from pure and untainted sources'. This view was echoed by Thomas Gray, a former Registrar-General of Seamen, who considered that although 'not more than 200,000 persons of all conditions are actually employed on British registered ships, and that little more than a moiety of these are seamen [in the specific rather than the generic sense] there can be no reason why all the boys reared up to maintain this – an insignificant fraction of our population – should not be derived from a *good* source instead of the outcasts of society'.

The Marine Society's *Warspite*, though lumped together with the other 'Independent Ships', maintained a clear view of its own strategy, mindful of the traditional redemptive aspect of its policy. It was, however, in one of its periodic financial crises, lack of funds in 1862 limiting the intake to 'only 140' boys and with the threat of the sale of the adjacent yard and its 'swimming-bath'. Indeed, the financing of such institutions became a bone of contention, though a sort of public-private initiative suggested funding them as general educational establishments, training ships for the merchant service and naval gunnery schools. Prominent and socially well-disposed ship-owners in Liverpool, particularly the Holt family, were broadly in favour of making a contribution, but in London 'there is no place in the world where the ship-owners act so entirely by themselves. They are a rope of sand. In Liverpool, if any public measure were about to be carried out, the ship-owners would combine to carry it.' This 'want of unanimity' scuppered the project and matters went on in piecemeal fashion. The complexities of the numbers of boys in sea-going training as apprentices being conditional upon the binding of young men to service in the Royal Naval Reserve only muddied the murky waters of capitalist enterprise, philanthropic or not.

In 1874 George Ward Hunt MP, the First Lord of the Admiralty, was the inspecting officer. He also had the duty of presenting the annual prizes.

A VICTORIAN SAILOR: JOSEPH RICHARD WOODMAN

Interviewed for The Daily Mail, *Brisbane, Sunday, 5 August, 1917*

"Yes, I am a member of the Queensland Naval Association. Like many Australians I was born in London where I should have perished rather than prospered if matters had not taken a turn for the better for I was in difficulties as a boy, though I had the knack of reading and writing. Luckily I was sent aboard The Marine Society's old ship, the *Venus*, that was on 25 August 1853. Funny name for a ship full of eager boys but they taught us the prime business of a seaman and that autumn we marched in the Lord Mayor's procession. I was sixteen. In December I signed-on and joined the collier-brig *Sarah Milledge* bound to the Baltic with coal. We boys received shocking hard treatment and I ran away from her. The Crimean War had begun and I entertained a foolish desire to see action, so I joined the Royal Navy.

That was in '55 and I was rated mizen topman in HMS *St George*. We didn't sail to the Black Sea though. Instead we undertook special duties, escorting the Royal Yacht to Boulogne when the old Queen visited Napoleon III and Empress Eugenie in Paris. After that we went to Lisbon for the coronation of the King of Portugal. Next year I transferred into the *Calcutta*. She was flagship of Vice Admiral Sir Michael Seymour and we went to Nagasaki in Japan; that would be about 1856 when the British ambassador concluded a Treaty of Commerce with the Mikado.

After this we sailed to Hong Kong and, there being trouble with the Chinese over the matter of opium, we bombarded the Bogue Forts at the mouth of the Pearl River that autumn and then took Canton. What a lark! A few months later we manned paddle-steamers, gun-boats and the fleet's pulling-boats and attacked a fleet of armed junks the Chinese had mustered in Fatshan Creek near Canton. I later took part in the attacks on the Taku forts in North China. We should have had troops to help us but they were diverted to India where the sepoy soldiers had mutinied. We had a lot of beer which had been shipped out for the army and Sir Michael decided it should be issued to us blue-jackets. This was all very well, but they gave it to us instead of our rum ration, which was very unpopular.

By 1860 I was back in England but had no luck and in 1882 I came out again to Queensland, to work as a fitter in the sugar mills in Mackay. This was not much to my liking so I signed on the Orient steamer *Liguria* as an Able Seaman and headed home. A year later I was back. I took up some land in Townsville. It was covered in the Prickly Pear, so I turned-to and developed Woodman's Liquid Cacticide with which I eradicated the blooming thing. I got neither credit not reward, though others used it to good effect.

But I gave it up and came to Brisbane in 1907. Three years ago I had to return to London to have my eyes seen to… The poisonous cacticide d'you see…

Well, there's another war now and our boys have been shipped off in the Anzac Corps and all the women are sending socks and chocolate. Huh! Socks and chocolate! We hadn't all the women folk knitting socks for us, and they didn't send us any chocolates or cigarettes either. Fancy chocolates and cigarettes for fighting men! It's them with cold feet that stay at home and hold up the veranda posts that want the warm socks and chocolates."

And the old fellow went off with a shake of the head at the thought of it all.

Joseph Richard Woodman, a Marine Society boy of 1853 with his "Cacticide" for eradicating the Prickly Pear in Australia.

Unaware of such matters, the boys aboard the training ships daily underwent a remarkably similar regime, only the education curricula marking the differences between the public-school cadets of the *Worcester*, the *Warspite*'s boys and the bad-lads in the 'Reformatories'. Routine, on board ship and in society at large, sustained the nation, and a contingent of Marine Society boys, led by their fife and drum band, regularly marched in the Lord Mayor of London's annual inaugural procession. Most of the boys taken up by the Society at this time had been in employment, though a few were entered 'from school'. The variety of the intake indicates the labour-intensive nature of mid-Victorian society, for boys were meticulously listed in the registers as having been sash-line makers, rope spinners, sofa-stuffers, French-polishers and so forth, though the majority had had more menial yet energetic jobs for which their youth fitted them: butchers'-, kitchen-, errand-, pot- and hawk-boys, the latter hawking their masters' wares about London's teeming streets. Few had been apprenticed and if they had 'a trade' they were only ancillary to it. One such was William Paul, who gave his employment as 'tailoring' rather than 'a tailor'. Many were presented to the Society by guardians such as uncles whose forbearance and sense of responsibility had perhaps been tested beyond endurance, though several listed as 'comedians' might have found treading the stages of the music-halls too uncertain a living for extended avuncular philanthropy. Other boys were surrendered by their indigent mothers, either widowed or single. Occasionally there is a whiff of vengeance: in September 1854 'the Mother of C. Callcott called [upon the Society] to say that her son's name is Mills, that being his father's name', while another was entered with the note that his 'Father [was] absconded, supposed dead.' Thus orphans and bastards, the victims of a pitiless social order and hapless all, came to The Marine Society to be taken in.

Perhaps in their uniforms, marching behind their mascot and their flag at the Lord Mayor's annual procession, they felt matters stood fair for their futures, though not all were appreciative of the Society's beneficence. Secured at her moorings in January 1876, the flammable old wooden-wall *Warspite* caught fire and, despite the attendance of the Southwark and Rotherhithe steam fire-floats, was burned out. It says much for the discipline of the ship's standing officers and her transient company of 220 boys that all were evacuated without loss of life. The fire started on the evening of 3 January, a Sunday when routine was relaxed. Significantly it followed the burning of the *Goliath* off Grays on 22 December. Naturally it was thought that 'the calamity following so soon [was] malicious'. The boys, it was noted by the Society's Secretary, Whitchurch Sadler, 'are not of a choice character when they join, petty offences, truant, aversion to work', and two of them were suspected of setting fire to the forward cockpit.

Fortunately, the Admiralty again promptly put another vessel at the Society's disposal. This was HMS *Clio*, a temporary expedient while a proper replacement was found and brought round to the Thames. HMS *Conqueror*, a 120-gun First Rate, three-decked ship-of-the-line, came up river in the following year, 1877. She had been launched at Chatham in 1833 as *Waterloo* and boasted a fine figurehead of the Duke of Wellington. In 1859 she had been fitted with a steam engine and became a screw line-of-battleship, metamorphosing in 1862 into HMS *Conqueror* and serving with Sir Michael Seymour's Far East Fleet in the late 1850s. Finally taken out of naval service in 1876, she passed by way of a refit to The Marine Society and underwent yet another renaming ceremony on 21 June 1877, when the Prince and Princess of Wales paid a visit to Woolwich and rechristened her *Warspite*.

This was an important occasion for the Society in more ways than one. Not only did the Admiralty allow the Society to continue using the name *Warspite* for their training ship, but another warrant granted the privilege of flying a blue ensign defaced in the lower fly canton with the Society's seal. The ceremony also allowed the Society to invite many of its well-to-do sponsors to board the new ship and see at first hand the work they supported. 'A private Steam Vessel', Whitchurch Sadler informed all those invited, 'will be engaged for the convenience of guests' to convey them from Charlton Pier to the ship. The royal party was well attended as it swept downstream in a fast steam-boat to the ship off Woolwich Dockyard. 'The shipping in the Pool and the Trinity launches at Blackwall were gay with flags', and on the approach of Their Royal Highnesses, the boys swarmed into *Warspite*'s rigging and manned the yards while a band played the National Anthem in the adjacent dockyard and a battery of horse artillery thundered a royal salute. A guard of honour was provided by boys with drawn cutlasses as the fifth Earl of Romney, his countess and the committee members welcomed the Prince and Princess.

> A fleet of steamers with flags flying had gathered round the vessel, and the dockyard was thronged with ladies and other spectators, who occupied seats on the timber strewn about. It became a cloudy day later on, but at that moment the sun was shining on the smart young sailors of the *Warspite*, who looked, in their clean white and blue uniforms, as if the change from London streets to a training-ship had done them good.

Having taken station on the poop, the royal party watched as:

> At the sound of the trumpet, followed by the shrill whistle of the boatswain, the lads ran aft with the halliards to make sail. They shortened and furled sail at the command of Captain Phipps, and then marched round the ship, 230 strong, to the music of their own drum and fife band playing "The British Grenadier." Their big black dog Neptune ran in front, led by a negro boy who had been found destitute in the docks and sent to The Marine Society for shelter and instruction. After this there was play (fencing) with single stick, and then the boys gathered aft, and while three of them held the flags drooping forward, the rest sang the … hymn "In darkness and in danger, on life's troubled sea."

This, *The Illustrated London News* recorded, was followed by a prize-giving when some received 'books of travel and adventure, knives, and warm monkey-jackets … from the gracious hands of the Princess of Wales'. The festivities continued with an address by the Prince before a grand luncheon was served at which subscriptions were announced. The Prince remarked pointedly to his audience that there was room on board the ship for 100 more boys if the money could be raised. Having inspected the ship, the royal party left to cannon fire and the boys singing ' "God Bless the Prince of Wales", the voices of those on the yards striking the ear as a sort of echo which came after the song of the boys below. Cheers were given at the close, which were caught up by the people congregated on the boats and wharves around, and the cannon fired a parting salute.' Such events were great occasions for the boys and served as useful platforms for fund raising, as did the annual inspection and an annual dinner, usually held at the Trafalgar Tavern, Greenwich, entrance to which in 1862 was one guinea.

Among the alumni of *Warspite* towards the end of the nineteenth century was 'the last impressionist', Frank Budgen, who served at sea in the 1890s. Later settling in Hampstead as a model, he afterwards went to Paris as an art student where he became a close friend of James Joyce.

An invitation to the inauguration of the Society's second *Warspite* by HRH The Prince of Wales in June 1877.

Although it was painfully slow and always imperfect, the wider social care of the seafarer, and hence many of The Marine Society's former trainees, continued to improve. Except in the most prestigious liner companies, conditions in the vast majority of merchant ships for both officers and ratings, whether employed on deck or in the engine compartments, were grim. Pay was poor and, particularly in the mid-1920s, frequently below the subsistence level. The various institutions catering for the welfare of seafarers struggled on. Like The Marine Society, which continued to seek donations and legacies and to manage its investments with due care, all the charitable institutions depended upon the generosity of the public at large and on the occasional bequest. The Society was to become increasingly intimate with many of the charities with which at first it simply co-existed.

In 1882 what had been the Asylum but was now more sensitively known as the Destitute Sailors' Rest – Asylum having come to mean something more specific – was moved to Gravesend, and a few years later the previous property was sold. In 1886 a new Sailors' Home was also opened in the town and a steam-launch, the *Maude*, was purchased to carry paid-off seamen directly to the Home. This spared them the temptation to head straight for a public-house only to fall into the hands of unscrupulous crimps, and enabled them if they wished to bank the bulk of their paying-off money in safe hands. Seven years later, the

The *Warspite*'s drum and fife band, *c.*1900.

Sailors' Home in Dock Street was modified to house 312 beds, and part of the site was used to connect with 18 Ensign Street, where new Mercantile Marine Offices, including the masters and mates examination hall and examiners' rooms, were now housed. Training was extended to improve the standard of food in many tramp ships by the establishment of the London School of Nautical Cookery in 1893. This had been initiated by the Sailors' Home Trust and was set up in the basement of the London Sailors' Home, which in 1912 was renamed the Sailors' Home and Red Ensign Club, to make it less institutional and more socially congenial.

Meanwhile the *Warspite* had quietly tugged at her moorings off Woolwich until she was moved downstream in 1901 to Greenhithe, where she lay while some of her boys embarked upon the adventure of a lifetime. In 1890 Lord Brassey and the ship-owner Sir Thomas Devitt of Devitt & Moore joined forces under what became known as The Brassey Scheme, to commission the commercial full-rigged ships *Harbinger* and *Hesperus* as sail-training ships for midshipmen, or officer-cadets who required sea time under sail to sit for their certificates of competence. Although, thanks to such facilities as the navigation classes at the Sailors' Home in Dock Street, it was possible for an able seaman to study and pass his Board of Trade examinations as a mate, it was a difficult and solitary task that ran counter to the culture of the forecastle. Moreover, the number of British nationals shipping as seamen was dwindling, ship-owners favouring cheaper manpower available abroad. In 1904 there were 39,832 'foreigners' under the red ensign and this did not include large numbers of Lascar and Chinese ratings well established in British ships. The number of boys signing indentures as apprentices fell significantly to only 5,179 in 1904. Concern over the influx of foreign men, whose loyalty might prove dubious in time of trouble, was widespread. In September 1904 *The Windsor Magazine*, an illustrated monthly publication for men and women, bemoaned the situation: 'Not only is the scarcity of British seamen a menace to our merchantmen, but, more seriously still, it threatens our Navy with the extinction of a source of supply which yields a most useful class of Naval Reserve … . In the face of this ever-increasingly perilous position … the Marine Society's own training ship *Warspite*, "through lack of pecuniary support," forsooth, can only undertake the training of 200 boys at a time, instead of her full complement of 300'.

The general unpopularity of apprenticeships in spite of their best efforts did not deter Brassey and Devitt from approaching The Marine Society with a new scheme. For their part, Devitt & Moore purchased a fine, iron four-masted barque, the *Port Jackson* of 2,212 gross tons, which had been built at Hall's Aberdeen yard in 1882. The vessel was to earn her keep on the London to Australia service, manned by a professional crew plus 100 *Warspite* boys, aged between 14 and 18, under training. It was felt that such an experience would prove successful in recruiting *British* boys and improving the general quality of the British seaman. It also gave practical expression to the fact that, as *The Windsor Magazine* pointed out, 'There is no profession under the sun that can boast so many self-made men as the Mercantile Marine … . There are no limits to promotion, as in the Navy, and a lad who goes to sea as a "deck hand" may, and often does, by perseverance and industry eventually achieve the summit of a sailor's ambition – the command of one of our palatial liners.' The *Port Jackson*'s voyage would put the feet of 100 youngsters on the first step of achievement.

On 21 May 1906, under Captain G. P. Ward, with three mates, Dr Beale from the London Hospital, the Revd Leonard Star of the Missions to Seamen, a Chief Instructor Glynn and two assistants, six cooks and stewards, four quartermasters, a boatswain, sail-maker, carpenter and fourteen able seamen, the *Port Jackson* left the South West India Dock bound for Sydney with a general cargo. The *Warspite* boys lined her rails but her departure was less dignified than anticipated, as she damaged her hull when she passed through the locks. Unfortunately, after repairs, her troubles were not yet over for she was obliged to anchor in The Downs owing to dense fog. It was here that she was run into by the German steam-ship *Pyrgos*.

As the bow of the *Pyrgos* drove deep into the *Port Jackson*'s fore part and the big barque heeled under the impact, the boys showed their mettle. Chief Instructor Glynn ordered the bugler to sound off the still. In the silence, with every boy standing to attention just as if they had been aboard the *Warspite* at her moorings, the order was given for 'Divisions to fall in on the deck house'. Although serious, the damage was all above the waterline and Captain

The formal prize-giving by HRH Princess Alexandra of Wales in 1877 at the inauguration of the new *Warspite*.
The Illustrated London News.

Sketches drawn on board *Warspite* during the inaugural visit of The Prince and Princess of Wales in 1877 to the second Marine Society ship to bear the name.
The Illustrated London News.

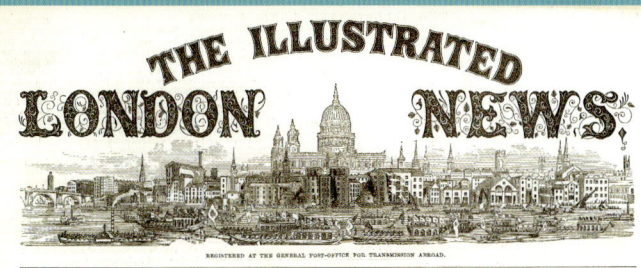

THE ILLUSTRATED LONDON NEWS

No. 1981.—VOL. LXX. SATURDAY, JUNE 30, 1877. WITH TWO SUPPLEMENTS SIXPENCE By Post, 6½d.

THE PRINCESS OF WALES PRESENTING THE PRIZES TO THE BOYS ON BOARD THE TRAINING-SHIP WARSPITE, AT WOOLWICH.

SUPPLEMENT TO THE ILLUSTRATED LONDON NEWS, JUNE 30, 1877.—617

SKETCHES ON BOARD THE TRAINING-SHIP WARSPITE, AT WOOLWICH, DURING THE VISIT OF THE PRINCE AND PRINCESS OF WALES.

Ward did not have to abandon the ship, but the *Port Jackson* had to return to the South West India Docks, where the damage was made good. She dropped downstream again on 25 June to anchor off Greenhithe where the *Warspite*'s band came aboard and gave a concert. Three days later, the tug *Oceana* finally took her in charge and towed her to sea, the pilot leaving off Start Point on 3 July.

The *Port Jackson*'s passage was not fast: she crossed the Line on 11 August, sighted Tristan da Cunha on 9 September and passed the meridian of the Cape of Good Hope on the 20 September. By 13 October she was south of Cape Leeuwin, entered Sydney Harbour on 1 November and was then towed alongside a berth at Woolloomooloo to discharge. The boys were entertained ashore, having Christmas dinner at the Mission to Seamen. After dry-docking, the *Port Jackson* loaded bales of wool, casks of tallow and government stores, and sailed for home on 10 January 1907. On 14 February she doubled Cape Horn, crossed the Equator on 14 March, made her number to Lloyd's Signal Station on the Lizard at eight in the morning of 16 April, and on 20 April she anchored below Greenhithe, one hundred days out from Sydney.

The costs of the voyage had been considerable and it did not prove profitable. In addition to outfitting the boys at £30 each, the Society, its resources limiting it to assisting only 220 boys in total, had only been able to raise £2,500 towards the exceptional additional costs of the voyage. Consequently Devitt and Moore decided that they must embark officer-cadets on the *Port Jackson*'s next voyage.

In the end a compromise was reached, and twenty-two cadets from the *Illawarra* were taken aboard, along with fifty *Warspite* boys. Captain Charles Maitland, late of the *Illawarra*, which had just been sold, took over from Ward, and a former Union Castle master, Captain Brackenbury, joined as nautical instructor. Leaving on 7 October, the *Port Jackson* 'had a magnificent sail down the coast, making an average of 10 knots and doing 13 at times' wrote Philip Devitt who, as part owner of the ship and a Marine Society committee member, took passage to Brixham. 'A tramp steamer, which had passed us when we were in tow off Beachy Head, got about two miles ahead, but as soon as we had clapped on all sail we quickly

Devitt & Moore's handsome four-masted barque *Port Jackson* in a light breeze. She was built by Hall of Aberdeen in 1882 for the firm of Duthie Bros.

passed her and left her a long way astern.' Devitt disembarked with the pilot and left the big barque to stand across towards Ushant. Once heading across the Bay of Biscay, the *Port Jackson* encountered a severe south-westerly gale but she weathered this and might have made a good passage but for the head wind she encountered as she approached her destination. She took 103 days to reach Sydney on 18 January 1908. For her homeward passage she loaded 10,000 bales of wool, 600 tons of concentrates, furs, skins and maize, then completed her lading with Admiralty explosives, leaving on 1 March. She reached the London River in ninety-five days, entering dock on the 5 June. The following week, accompanied by their fife and drum band and under the command of *Warspite*'s captain-superintendent, Commander W. H. F. Montanaro, the fifty boys paraded at Marlborough House and were addressed by the Prince of Wales. Within eight weeks of their return all the boys were drafted, forty-six joining merchantmen and four the Royal Navy.

Sadly, this was the last time the *Port Jackson* bore upon her books any Marine Society boys, though she continued to train officer-cadets. In economic terms, the experiment had been a failure, which was a pity, for of the 100 boys who sailed on the first voyage no fewer than 94 had immediately signed on as ordinary seamen in the mercantile marine, eight of them in sailing ships. Another twenty-one had joined the Cunard Line and the rest had signed on in tramp steamers at £2 per month; the remaining six joined the Royal Navy.

An appeal to underwrite the costs of future voyages foundered under public apathy but, to its credit, The Marine Society navigated through these troubled waters, keeping up its self-imposed duty among the nation's less fortunate youth and, in its way, giving them the means to advance their careers further than the forecastle if they possessed the character and aptitude. The Society was helped by many donations, particularly the gift from a Mr G. H. P. Livesay of the *Ernest*, a 25-ton 'dandy-rigged' ketch which provided the *Warspite* with a fine sailing tender for many years.

Lying off Greenhithe, a relic of a past age, the second *Warspite* produced young ratings destined to go down to the sea in the castles of steel that had succeeded the wooden walls. But these had not been forgotten and, while the Royal Navy was preparing for a new Trafalgar against the Kaiser's Germany, with which Great Britain had for some years been locked into an arms race, Nelson's great battle was remembered. In 1905, as the Society for Nautical Research was founded to save HMS *Victory* for the nation in the centenary year of Trafalgar, a loose alliance of philanthropists, churchmen, ship-owners and brokers, and including The Marine Society, decided to commemorate Nelson's victory and to draw the nation's attention to its continuing obligation to its seafaring community by instituting an Annual Seafarers' Service. By permission of the Dean and Chapter, this has been held ever since in St Paul's cathedral, above the admiral's mortal remains in the crypt below, in October, the month of his great triumph.

In the years following 1907, when serious rearmament began with the launch of the revolutionary battleship HMS *Dreadnought*, The Marine Society once again outfitted some 550 men. Its contribution to the Royal Navy between 1862 and 1918 was to be 3,689 boys, and to the merchant service a further 9,928. The Society continued to attract notice, with its annual inspections a feature of fashionable life. The Royal Dukes of Edinburgh and Cambridge, Prince Arthur of Connaught, several First Lords of the Admiralty, and admirals Lords Brassey and Beresford, the Lord Bishop of Rochester, several Lord Mayors of London and Deputy Masters of Trinity House, the Chairmen of the Peninsular and Oriental Steam Navigation Company and of the Royal Mail Line, the historian Herbert Fisher, all at some time filled the office of chief inspector. In 1913 Admiral Prince Louis of Battenberg, then First Sea Lord, played his part; and not for the first time leading journalists, with characteristic inaccuracy, reported the event as an inspection of The 'Royal' Marine Society.

The First World War did not yield the Royal Navy a second Trafalgar; instead it suffered terrible losses in the Pyrrhic victory of Jutland. And while the Grand Fleet successfully denied the German High Seas Fleet access to the oceans to which it aspired, German submarines wrought truly appalling havoc among the British mercantile marine. In fact, the U-boats came within a whisker of victory, for in 1917 the Admiralty reported to the government that they were losing the war at sea through their inability to protect the merchant fleet. Only the immediate introduction of convoys stopped the haemorrhage of ships, among them the *Port*

Jackson, and men, among whom many former Marine Society boys were numbered. Others served in the army and one, Sergeant Arthur Saunders, won a Victoria Cross. Attempts by the authorities to ameliorate the sufferings of torpedoed seamen led in 1917 to the establishment of King George's Fund for Sailors, for which The Marine Society's committee members lobbied actively.

At this critical time, as the mercantile marine was moulded by war into a fourth service of national importance, soon to be more commonly known as the 'merchant navy', the state finally took a major stake in the training and welfare of seafarers. In 1917 the newly established

The *Port Jackson*, her main yards aback as she lies hove-to, awaits the approach of a boat.

Jack Spurling, 1925.

Ministry of Shipping took over both the Sailors' Home and the Destitute Sailors' Rest at Gravesend, turning the premises over to sea-training. This process was formalised in 1921 when the *Vindicatrix* was commissioned as the National Sea Training School.

The second *Warspite* was also a casualty at this time, though not of enemy action. On the afternoon of Sunday 20 January 1918, like her predecessor and the *Goliath*, she too caught fire. Smoke was discovered rising from her coal bunkers, coal being used to heat the ship and fire the galley range. Strenuous efforts were made to stem the flames and assistance was called for as the ship filled with smoke. At 1715 'Abandon Ship' was sounded on the bugle and the boys were evacuated to the *Worcester* by way of the ship's cutters. Several boys had distinguished themselves by their attempts to extinguish the fire, in particular Gourd and Seaman, both of whom were nearly asphyxiated. Efforts by a number of fire-floats and tugs, together with assistance from the Shaftesbury Homes ship *Arethusa*, though gallant, were ineffectual. The fire raged unchecked until about 2200 when the *Warspite*'s officers finally gave up the unequal struggle. At 2300 the main mast fell and with it, the Society's pendant.

In the end the *Warspite* sat on the bottom and the rising tide did the rest. At low water she lay a wreck, her waist a broken mass of charred futtocks, her bow all that was recognisable, with its figurehead of the Iron Duke canted at a disagreeable angle. Meanwhile, all hands had been mustered as present aboard *Worcester*, temporarily emptied of the officer-cadets by the Christmas holiday. Despite, or perhaps because of, what was learnt later, their

The Society's second *Warspite* and her sailing tender *Ernest*. Note the boys at sail drill on the fore and main top and topgallant yards.

Wash-deck routine aboard the second *Warspite* in 1911.

discipline and behaviour had been impeccable, although they lost all their meagre personal possessions.

Although spontaneous combustion was considered the cause, rumours quickly circulated that again the devil had found work for idle hands on a Sunday. It was an open secret that a large number of boys were aware of a conspiracy to set fire to the ship and many admitted to having collected flammable material. They were all interviewed aboard *Worcester* by a Sergeant Binfield from Swanscombe Police Station. Binfield had little difficulty in identifying those responsible for setting fire to this kindling. At an initial hearing at Gravesend Magistrates' Court, Ernest Adams and Harold Gurr, both 14, and Frederick Blogg, 15, were charged with arson. Oil had been stolen from one of the ship's boat's navigation lamps and

Blogg had used matches hidden in his jersey to ignite some old canvas and wood in the fore part of the ship. Before the magistrates they made allegations of ill-usage and 'the court was told of the general feeling of unrest and resentment against the harsh disciplinary measures of the ship's officers and petty officers causing a very high proportion of the trainees to be implicated'. The three boys were convicted at Kent Assizes on 16 February and sentenced to three years in a Reformatory.

Meanwhile, the complement of 240 boys had been resettled, most of them aboard HMS *President III*. This ship had been, as she was later, the RNVR drill ship, and she lay at moorings near Blackfriars. The *Warspite*'s captain-superintendent, Captain A. G. K. Hill RN, took temporary command, hoisting the Society's pendant and ensign. The rest of the boys were put up in the Tilbury Hotel, which the Society leased, and later some of the seniors destined for the navy were transferred straight away to HMS *Impregnable*. Owing to the war and its aftermath, the Society was obliged to continue with the unsatisfactory expedient of the Tilbury Hotel for some time.

In 1919 Captain Charles Lenny RN became secretary of the Society. He had gone to sea in sail 1886 and did not turn to steam until he had his Extra Master's certificate, when he joined the Royal Naval Reserve as a sub-lieutenant. Two years later he transferred to the regular navy and 'after varied service did four years as assistant to the King's Harbour Master at Devonport before joining the Coastguard'. On retiring from the navy he was appointed to The Marine Society and in 1922 was instrumental in the purchase of a new training-ship, the old Second-class Protected Cruiser *Hermione*. Built at Devonport in 1893, *Hermione* had taken part in the suppression of the Boxer Rising in China and in 1910 had worked with naval dirigibles. After refitting for training, a refit that included removing her twin funnels, she too was renamed *Warspite* – although there was a battleship in the Royal Navy with the same ancient name – and as before, was inaugurated by the then Prince of Wales (afterwards the Duke of Windsor) on 24 July 1923. In 1929 her mooring was deemed to inhibit the navigable channel, though rumour suggested that this judgement was reached largely through a subterfuge. As legend has it, Arthur Goodwin, a skipper of one of F. T. Everard's sailing barges, deliberately fouled his bowsprit in *Warspite*'s moorings to 'prove' that the training-ship obstructed the approach to Everard's Greenhithe wharf and was interfering with the company's business. Goodwin was said to have been acting on Everard's instructions, but whatever the truth, the third *Warspite* was moved further downstream to Tilbury Reach and shackled to moorings off Grays, some distance from the yard and swimming-bath ashore. Here she was to train a generation of boys destined to serve in another war under successive captains-superintendent, Commanders L. H. Bayley and H. G. L. Harvey.

In 1932 another appeal was made for £8,000 'to defray expense of hospital, swimming bath and boat shed'. The boys, 'taken at the age of 14 ... are the future Sailors and as such may be the saviours of our Empire ... [and] are clothed, trained and maintained for about 12 months in an atmosphere of LOYALTY and DISCIPLINE. Only boys', the appeal concluded, 'of GOOD CHARACTER are admitted. There are over 200 on board but there is accommodation for another 100, if funds were available. PLEASE HELP!!'

In 1913 Admiral Prince Louis of Battenberg was First Sea Lord and inspected the *Warspite*. Here he addresses the boys assembled on deck.

Although the regime remained spartan, the day's routine beginning at 0530 in the summer, with school and seamanship occupying approximately equal periods in the timetable, due emphasis was laid upon keeping the ship clean and the boys fit. On Friday afternoons, a half-holiday was given, and the lads went ashore, to pay for it on Saturday when the whole ship was thoroughly scrubbed. Drill was practised every Tuesday and Wednesday afternoon, and a period for recreation was permitted in the early evening. Morning Service was held by the chaplain every Sunday, though he gave 'religious instruction' four times a week and Holy Communion once a month. Confirmation classes were undertaken with each annual draft and culminated in a laying-on of hands by the Lord Bishop of Rochester.

As before, each boy was supplied on entry with an outfit that now consisted of two blue serge jerkins, a Guernsey, two pairs of blue cloth trousers, two flannel and three striped

The sad remains of the burnt-out *Warspite*, March 1918, viewed from astern.

The Illustrated London News.

A guard drawn up aboard the second *Warspite* in 1911.

The looming bulk of the Society's second *Warspite* seen at sunset in Lionel Wyllie's painting, *c.*1902, must have seemed a forbidding home for a new boy. The tender *Ernest* is on the *Warspite*'s port side.

William Lionel Wyllie.

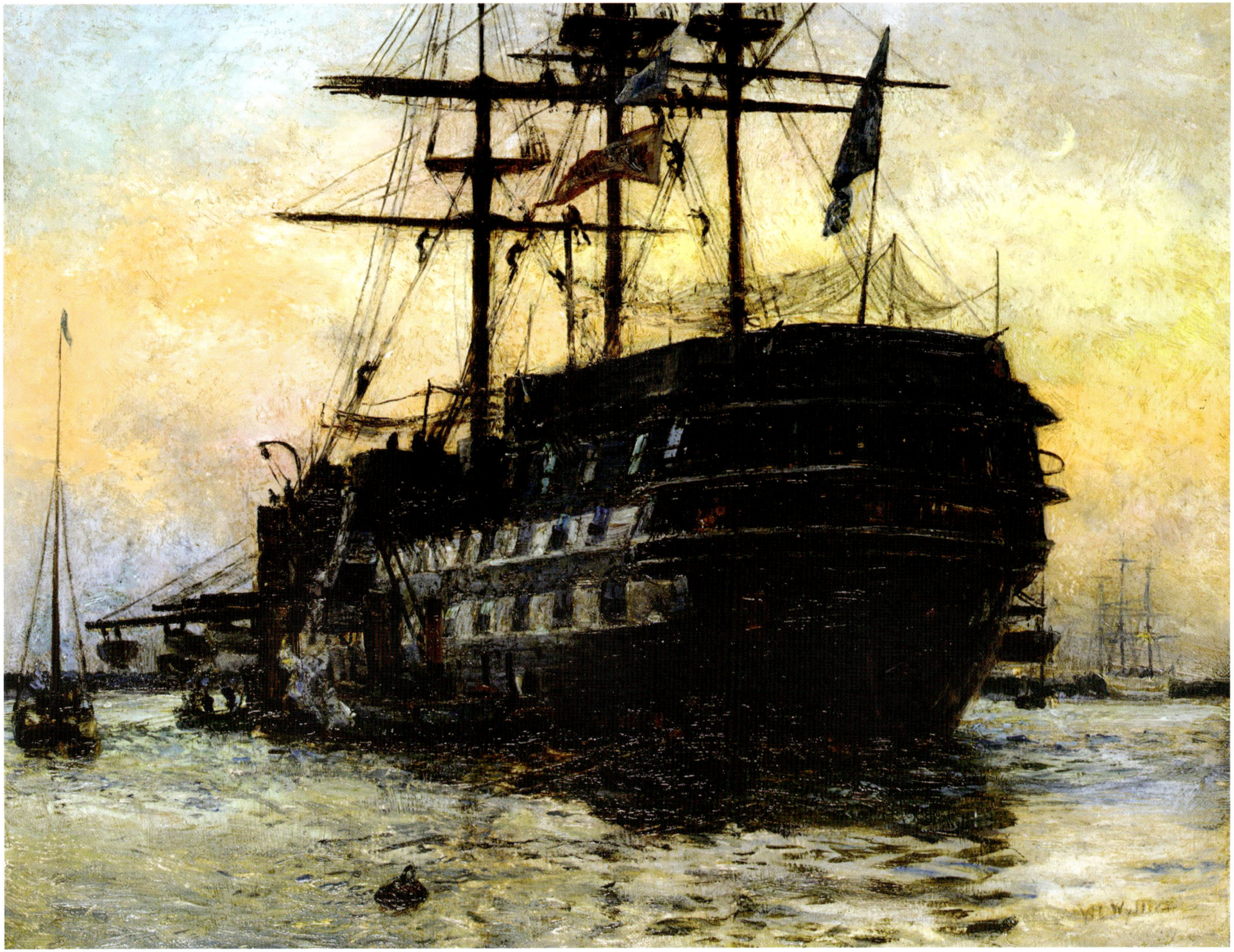

cotton shirts, two pairs of worsted socks, two pairs of boots, a silk handkerchief, two blue and one white caps, a towel and two flannels, all of which stowed inside a black-painted canvas bag. A hammock, mattress, pillow and blanket, plus toothbrush, clothes brush and mending materials in a hussif completed the inventory, and all had to be mustered for regular Divisional inspections. In February 1933 the three cotton shirts were withdrawn and a pullover was issued in lieu for the winter months. After six months, additional socks and other items were replaced and a tie was added; upon discharge a trainee took his kit with him, the Society adding a dungaree suit, extra socks and shirts, a set of oilskins including a sou'wester, a plate, knife and fork and, of course, the Bible and a prayer book.

Even without her funnels the Society's third and last *Warspite* **dressed overall, her boats alongside, makes an imposing sight at her moorings.**
The Lloyd Mail.

Personal documentation of a Marine Society boy, Ronald William Capp, recording his dates of training, ability and conduct, plus the fact that he was fit and vaccinated for sea-service.

No. 30

MARINE SOCIETY'S TRAINING SHIP "WARSPITE."
GRAYS, ESSEX.

CERTIFICATE OF ABILITY AND CONDUCT.

NAME IN FULL.	DATE OF BIRTH.
Ronald William Capp	15 July 1923

RATING AND BADGES ON COMPLETION OF TRAINING.	HEIGHT ON DISCHARGE 5 ft. 2 in.
Leading Seaman Two G.C. Badges	COLOUR OF EYES: Blue — HAIR: Fair — COMPLEXION: Fresh

This is to Certify that the above-named boy having been accepted for training on board this Ship, on completion of the same is discharged to the Society's Shipping Agent for draft to sea, this 14th day of October 1938.

During his course of training he has been instructed in the elementary duties of a seaman.

Conduct VG   Ability VG
School   Upper   Swimming Yes
Other Qualifications Trained as Captain Superintendent's Cook

Remarks Admitted 23-9-37

[signature]
Captain, R.N., Captain-Superintendent.

CERTIFICATE FOR PRESENTATION ON FIRST SHIPMENT ONLY

No. 30

MARINE SOCIETY'S TRAINING SHIP "WARSPITE."
GRAYS, ESSEX.

The Officer receiving this Certificate is particularly requested not to hand it back to the boy mentioned therein, who has received a duplicate. This Certificate should be destroyed when finished with.

CERTIFICATE OF ABILITY AND CONDUCT.

[duplicate of the above]

Training Ship "WARSPITE."

Certified that I have this day vaccinated R. W. Capp and I find that he is quite fit to go to sea.

Date 15-10-37

[signature]
Medical Officer.

New entrants, who had to be sons of poor parents, joined *Warspite* under two-year indentures. Subject to medical fitness, the only real qualification an applicant required was evidence 'of a good character … <u>especially for honesty</u>'. The Society undertook to train applicants 'free of all expense to parents or guardians'. The boys could be discharged for naval service any time after receiving six months' training, in which case their indentures were cancelled, the remainder of their training being undertaken by the navy. Boys:

> not selected for the Royal Navy will go through a course of 12 to 15 months' training … . On the conclusion … all boys will be drafted to sea, and … will complete their apprenticeships in sea-going ships … . IT MUST BE CLEARLY UNDERSTOOD THAT THEY ARE SENT INTO THE SEA SERVICE SELECTED BY THE COMMITTEE, AND THAT THEY AND THEIR PARENTS HAVE NO CHOICE IN THE MATTER; THEY MUST REMAIN AT SEA UNTIL THEIR INDENTURES EXPIRE.

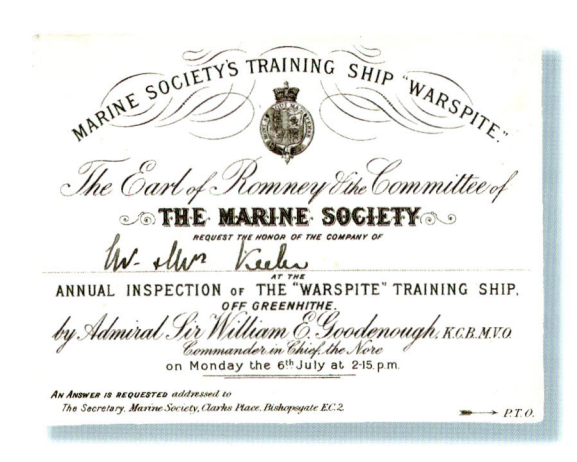

An invitation to board *Warspite* for the annual inspection, which in 1925 was conducted by Admiral Sir William Goodenough.

Another view of the old cruiser *Hermione* in her final incarnation as the Society's last *Warspite*.

After basic training, some boys were sent to the London School of Nautical Cookery at the Sailors' Home to qualify as sea cooks by Board of Trade examination.

In 1935, *Warspite*'s shore establishment was sold off and the figurehead of the Duke of Wellington, all that remained of the second *Warspite* and former *Waterloo*, was brought aboard and erected on the quarterdeck of *Warspite III* but subsequently migrated to New York. The 1935 Annual Court met at Clark's Place, Bishopsgate, under the chairmanship of Mr Frederick Mead, Lord Romney being absent on duty with the Coldstream Guards. Mead reported that 277 boys had been under training, with 176 admitted during the year. Of those leaving after their year on board, sixty-five were joining the navy, four of them in the Advanced Class; sixty-two were going into the mercantile marine. Two of the naval entrants, Judkins and Batten, had won the Admiralty's first and second prizes for boys coming from training establishments during 1934. This was gratifying to the committee, which had instituted its own awards system as part of their after-care policy. 'Old Boys' able to prove five years of good conduct were awarded the Society's Silver medal, an inscribed parchment and a gratuity. Those who reached warrant rank in the navy were given a sword, and those passing for second mate in the merchant navy a sextant, no mean gift for the aspirant concerned. The committee went further. 'Cases of misfortune are assisted' and 'Those out of employment are found a fresh berth', provisions most welcome to merchant mariners for whom such welfare was almost unheard of, though it was pointed out to boys joining the merchant navy that they would receive better remuneration at sea than normal apprentices and 'it is your duty to lay by and provide for yourself between voyages or when out of a ship'. However, those defaulting on their obligations 'may be sent back to the *Warspite* until their indentures expire'.

At this time the ship's staff consisted of a captain-superintendent, a chief officer, a head schoolmaster who doubled as purser, an assistant master who acted as bandmaster, a second officer who was also the master-at-arms and clothing storekeeper, a third officer who was seamanship and sail-making instructor, supported by two seamanship instructors. Most of these men came from the Royal Navy and between them provided a wide range of instruction

Commander L. H. Bayley RN, Captain-Superintendent of *Warspite***, poses in typical fashion with pet dog and telescope. Note the figurehead of Wellington belonging to the earlier** *Warspite* **and here erected on the deck of the former cruiser.**

including gunnery, physical exercise and swimming, electrical skills and carpentry. First-aid was taught by a sick-berth steward who also acted in this capacity when required and there were three night-watchmen. The sailing tender *Ernest* had an appointed officer-in-charge and mate, subsidiary duties of the seamanship instructors.

Within the *Warspite*, as in all static training-ships, a hierarchical system existed, with ranks and appointments for the boys themselves, encouraging a sense of responsibility and self-reliance. For example, many boys joined the choir or the band, while the *Ernest* could not proceed to sea without her 'permanent crew' which, besides the officer-in-charge and his mate, consisted of 'two Carpenter Boys and two Petty-Officer Boys'. Such petty-officer boys exercised especial responsibilities in sail drill or boat-work. Since the ship was tended by her own boats, plenty of adventures, and opportunities for demonstrating initiative, occurred to those sent away in them. The distance between the ship and the swimming baths made long boat trips part of everyday routine. Water and all necessary stores had to be brought out to the *Warspite* by boat, and things often went awry. The ship's printed *Log* contained accounts of all such japes, and one probably typical entry bemoaned a spell of gales and told of the jolly boat being blown onto the mud on her way back from 'the Baths'.

> The waves broke over her and her shivering crew until the tide finally left her high and dry … . They could not get her out on account of the mud … . However, a line was eventually thrown to them from the Wharf and with the generous help of the men working there they were towed bodily through the mud by a locomotive until they reached the Wharf … . With more aid from the engine [the boat] was eventually got afloat again and the crew, after having a warm up by the fire in the hut on the Wharf started back and arrived on board moist but hungry.

The Society's finances in 1935 showed a balance on the right side, but that had only been obtained by economy and the regrettable reduction of the number of boys under instruction. Overhead expenses were practically the same, whatever the number of boys on board, so

Originally fitted to HMS *Waterloo*, which became the second *Warspite*, the figurehead of the 'Iron Duke' was later set up ashore.

that fresh subscriptions had an enhanced economic value because the cost of victualling and clothing was the only extra, incidental to the maintenance of each additional boy.

As the world recovered from the Depression years 'The demand of ship-owners for *Warspite* boys being greater than the supply was another good ground for appeal to the benevolent public for further assistance.' Money was specifically needed for a new heated swimming-pool on board, the old yard and baths having now been sold, 'as no boy was sent to sea unless he could swim' and this was shortly afterwards installed.

Meanwhile, much else was afoot as interest in youth training became a matter of increasing public attention. Misgivings as to the general physique of the nation's young men had been expressed during the war by military doctors shocked at the poor constitution of those coming forward for military service. The quality of the potential soldiers who would guard and serve the British Empire and Commonwealth was perceived as a matter of national pride, particularly since a generation had been exterminated in the killing fields of Flanders. The Boy Scouts, Boys' Brigade and Church Lads' Brigade were the best known and most enduring of a number of organisations aimed at improving matters, particularly for urban youth. Several of these had been in existence for many years, like the Naval Lads' Brigades set up in naval ports by naval veterans who, returning from the Crimean War, taught maritime skills to poor boys. All these disparate organisations sought to promote self-reliance, discipline and quasi-military rituals, incorporating to a greater or lesser degree both imperial and Christian ideals.

The Navy League had been formed in 1894 as a lobbying organisation dedicated to reminding the country and Parliament of our national reliance upon the Royal Navy. By 1914 it had a subscribing membership of 100,000 and took up the sponsoring of many of the Naval Lads' Brigades as The Navy League Boys' Naval Brigade. Although the onset of war delayed matters, in 1919 these thirty-four brigades were granted Admiralty recognition as the Navy League Sea Cadet Corps. Each of the units, some of which had their own small training brigs, was to be subject to annual inspection by an officer from the staff of the Admiral Commanding Reserves. The remaining five smaller, 'unrecognised' cadet bodies were slowly subsumed. During the Depression, however, membership and subscriptions fell away, but at the annual dinner of The Navy League in 1937, when Winston Churchill gave the principal speech, it was announced that in addition to the funds the members themselves had raised, the philanthropist Lord Nuffield, head of Morris Motors Ltd, had donated £50,000. By the outbreak of war two years later, there were one hundred units in the country, each with its cadre of retired naval personnel, mustering more than 10,000 Sea Cadets. Coincidentally, their motto, 'Ready, Aye, Ready' could hardly have been more appropriate as once again the demands of war forced a massive expansion of the Royal Navy.

The Navy League was just one more example of the growing awareness of social responsibility, particularly with respect for seafarers. The socialist ideal had become almost a fashion among an intellectual élite, and was mixed with a robust and muscular Christianity aimed at improving the lot of the nation's poor. Immediately following the 1918 armistice, a boom in the world economy and an increased demand for shipping had seemed to promise a bright future, particularly for the newly self-conscious merchant navy which received its royal baptism from King George V in 1920. Unfortunately, within five years, the onset of a slump that was to plunge into the Depression following the Wall Street crash of 1929 made the task of social reform difficult to the point of impossibility. The extensive strikes that affected British shipping in 1925 led the government to take a tough line against the participants in the General Strike the following year, and the merchant navy, after its sacrifices in war, seemed destined not to live up to the image its patrons and proponents had designed for it.

Nevertheless, some far-sighted individuals remained undeterred, one such being a certain Albert Mansbridge, in his way as remarkable a man as Jonas Hanway. Born of working-class parents, Mansbridge won a scholarship to grammar school only to be forced to leave at 14 to earn a living, first as a government clerk, later as a warehouse clerk with the Co-operative Wholesale Society. A keen lay-member of the Anglican church, Mansbridge was also an eager contributor to the University Extension Journal, and the ideas he promulgated led in 1903 to the founding of what became the Workers' Educational Association and which attracted some of the finest scholars of the day as lecturers. Mansbridge, its first general

The Marine Society medal, presented to former *Warspite* boys for five years of exemplary service and still awarded annually for deeds of exceptional merit at sea.

Views of life aboard the third and final *Warspite* from *The Sphere* in 1936. *The Sphere*'s assumption that the trainees would join the Royal Navy was incorrect; many went into the merchant service.

TRAINING BOYS for the NAVY
Special "Sphere" Pictures taken on "Warspite"

KEEPING THEIR EYES ON THE BOARD: The ordinary education of the lads, with a special view to their future employment, is carried on in the class-rooms below decks and demands close attention in spite of the counter-fascination of the endless stream of shipping passing close alongside

In the Navy's present anxiety to get just the right type of boy for the new ships which are being built, and to convert him into an efficient man-of-warsman as quickly as possible, the various training ships are doing work that is beyond all praise, for they are taking the boy of good character and giving him a preliminary training which fits him admirably for the intensive work at the naval establishments at Shotley or Gosport. During the year or so *(Continued below on right)*

AT THE HELM: By means of this ingenious contrivance the budding quartermaster finds that it is not so difficult to steer a straight course as long as he does not let his attention wander, and keeps an eye on the compass card. You can depend, however, that all his messmates are quite sure they can do as well when it comes to their turn

THE SHIP'S CHAPEL: The Captain Superintendent taking prayers before the boys turn in for the night. *Warspite* also has a chaplain

HANDLING "WARSPITE'S" STORES: Senior boys demonstrating to the juniors the seemingly complicated art of knot tying when dealing with barrels of provisions

LOOKING AFT FROM THE BRIDGE: A scene on the deck of *Warspite*, which is moored in the Thames off Grays, Essex, showing in the background the boys drawn up as smartly as their seniors at divisions on board a man o' war. They are waiting to be told off to their various jobs

DINNER TIME: The new boys who have just arrived on board find the meals, served piping hot from the big galley in the middle of the mess deck, just to their taste after a strenuous morning at preliminary training, and the old hand who serves as general guide and "cook of the mess"—without doing any cooking—knows just what sized portions he is expected to serve when it comes to the plum duff with lots of plums. The food is excellent and plentiful, the authorities recognising the importance of sound nourishment

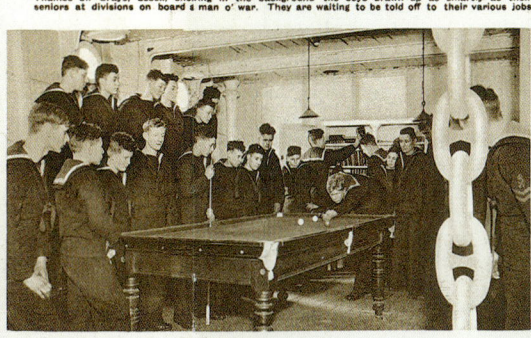

WOULD-BE LINDRUMS: Billiards is perhaps the most popular pastime for the leisure hours, but the library, seen in the background, is also well patronised

which he spends in the training ship he gets a thorough grounding of naval ways and thought, so that when he is drafted into the service proper he is already well prepared, and can assimilate the instruction very much more quickly and thoroughly than the boy who is entered straight from home. Also, and it is a very great advantage, he has had a foretaste of naval life and discipline, so that if he does not like them he has the chance of finding another vocation before he pledges himself irrevocably, and so avoids the chance of becoming one of the disgruntled bluejackets who can do infinite harm to the spirit of a mess, or even a "K.H.B." (King's Hard Bargain).

In this work the training ship *Warspite*, moored in the Thames off Grays, Essex, is maintaining a foremost position as befits the premier training ship in the country. She belongs to, and is maintained by, the Marine Society which was founded in 1756 by Jonas Hanway, one of the great characters in the eighteenth-century mercantile world. He invented the umbrella and started the crusade against boy chimney sweeps, but it is with the Marine Society that his name is most usually associated. In his day the fleet was manned very largely by the press gang and the mortality among the men who went to sea for an indefinite voyage with no more clothing than they were wearing when they were taken was terrible. Hanway's very practical idea was to raise a fund to give these men a reasonable kit, which not only reduced their hardships but gave

(Continued on page 472)

ORDERLY TO THE CAPTAIN SUPERINTENDENT, as he transacts the ship's business in his after-cabin, is a responsible job very much sought after by the boys who know that smartness and intelligence shown in it may lead to very good chances of promotion when they get to sea and already know the ropes. *Warspite* has sent hosts of fine lads both to the Navy and the Merchant Service

William Davis

secretary, rapidly became involved with the numerous bodies attempting to improve the lot of intelligent working people. He was a member of the Consultative Committee of the Board of Education, an adviser to the War Office on army education and a director of the Co-operative Building Society. Illness interposed, and in 1911 he was prescribed a recuperative voyage. Taking passage aboard the tramp-steamer *Venedotian*, he was deeply affected by the marginalised and bleak world of the merchant seaman. Other voyages were to follow, as he carried his message of education-for-all across the Empire while preaching the advantages of adult education, which, he believed, had 'a universal relevance … as an essential aspect of life in a democratic community'.

In 1918 Mansbridge founded the World Association for Adult Education, forerunner of the United Nations Educational, Scientific and Cultural Organisation, and 1919 he set up the Seafarers' Education Service, initially to provide British ships with a library of inspiring books. He went on to acquire a world-wide reputation as an energetic Christian reformer, a fact that endeared him to those in power who saw the need for social reform but were instinctively hostile to socialism and communism. Mansbridge believed that everyone possessed a unique skill or aptitude, exercise of which conferred happiness or at least a state of contentment, and if this skill or talent could be tapped it would be of benefit not only to the individual but to society at large. Education as a means of determining that individual

The smart sailing tender *Ernest* on the Thames.

Albert Mansbridge, pioneer in the education of the working man and founder of the Seafarers' Education Service.

Painted by his son, John Mansbridge.

excellence was to be the key to the Seafarers' Education Service which was, in the coming years, to offer instruction on all manner of subjects from atomic physics to zoology. By sheer force of personality Mansbridge, and his able successor as director, Dr Ronald Hope, were able to attract as volunteer tutors some of the most distinguished intellectuals of the age such that it was possible for a fireman aboard a tramp steamer to receive personal tuition in history from an Oxbridge don.

Mansbridge's first task in 1919 was to find a way of launching his Seafarers' Education Service and he found a willing ally in the paternalistic but enlightened Liverpool ship-owner Lawrence Holt, a manager of Alfred Holt & Company's Blue Funnel Line. On 29 May 1920 Holt's cargo-liner SS *Aeneas* sailed for Australia with a library of 150 books on board, supplied by the Seafarers' Education Service. The books were eagerly borrowed and read, and the library's solitary atlas was in constant demand. In contrast with workers ashore, seamen showed little interest in industrial history or economics, reserving their greatest enthusiasm for natural history. On the following voyage, *Aeneas* carried a library of 200 volumes and by her next trip about half of the ship's company were habitual readers, one third of the books were always out on loan and total loans exceeded one thousand. From this initial experiment, the provision of libraries became almost universal among British merchant ships, four hundred carrying libraries only ten years after the inauguration of the SES, as it became familiarly known.

Finance was, of course, a fundamental problem. The Director of the Seafarers' Education Service had of necessity to be a gymnastic fund-raiser, though the organisation had no appeals department. 'Flogging the idea of libraries to certain ship-owners was hard work,' Mansbridge's successor Ronald Hope recalled, 'work I didn't like. Many ship-owners didn't think it was necessary for their seamen to read.' Despite the difficulties, money was won or wheedled from various sources. Some, like the Ellerman and the Carnegie United Kingdom Trusts were helpful; other ship-owners and potential benefactors, anxious to get Mansbridge, and later Hope, out of their offices, made grants, donations and promises of bequests sufficient to fund this extraordinary and ultimately very successful concept. In 1926, Mansbridge

The Society's third and final *Warspite* seen from the port quarter.

secured 16 Russell Square, London, WC1 as the joint headquarters for the Seafarers' Education Service and the World Association for Adult Education. In 1938 the SES moved a short distance to Selwyn House (now Skepper House) in Endsleigh Street, where it was to remain until 1951.

On the outbreak of war in September 1939, the College of the Sea, a 1938 off-shoot of the SES, extended its remit to include the Royal Navy, many of whose 'Hostilities Only' ratings were young men whose university studies had been interrupted. Elsewhere the war had a different impact. As German air raids began, the lower Thames in which the *Warspite* lay was declared a danger zone. Consequently her 161 trainees were dispersed, most being sent to sea within months, others being supported by bursaries in Seamen's Homes until ships were found for them. The old cruiser lay empty and idle for a year until 16 September 1940 when she was sold to the ship-breakers T. W. Ward. Towed away on 2 October, her recycled steel was to contribute to the war effort.

Alfred Holt's Blue Funnel cargo-passenger liner SS *Aeneas* was the first British merchantman to carry a library provided by the SES.
B. and A. Fielden.

As in the First World War, many Marine Society boys were killed, one being lost with the *Jervis Bay*, three in the *Royal Oak* and four in the *Hood*. Yet another was lost on his first voyage to sea when his merchant ship was torpedoed, several were drowned or killed in air raids and two died in action serving with the Royal Air Force. Among others lost at sea, one former *Port Jackson* boy was killed when the paddle minesweeper *Snaefell* was bombed off Sunderland in July 1941.

Ironically, war, the very thing that had called The Marine Society into existence, ended its long tradition of training poor boys for sea careers. It had in total sent some 70,829 boys and 39,910 men and, although by combining with the Navy League in 1941 it helped 3,435 Sea Cadets pass through an induction course prior to joining the Royal Navy, its original *raison d'être* no longer existed. The wholesale conscription of the Second World War rendered the method of recruitment obsolete and, despite years of austerity, the reforming post-war Labour government and the Welfare State finally rendered the source defunct. Hanway, one imagines, would have been pleased at the union of charity and policy.

But there remained work to do, not least because the parlous conditions in which many merchant seamen existed demanded attention. A War Library Service was started; in 1936 a British Ship Adoption Society had been founded to link schools with merchant ships and in 1939, with Marine Society support, The Merchant Navy Comforts Service was established to provide clothing to merchant seamen. For, to their dismay, merchant seafarers lucky enough to survive enemy attack found on returning home that their pay had stopped the moment their ship was sunk and they were reduced to a humiliating indigence. Recognising the nation's ingratitude and injustice to a civilian service precipitated into the front line, the Comforts Service encouraged the provision of warm clothes, welcome to all surviving seamen but particularly so to those on ships diverted to Russia. The Service eventually proved an important contributor to keeping sufficient merchant seamen at sea to sustain 'the Atlantic bridge'.

In 1944, with the end of the war in sight, the Society's committee decided not to resuscitate the idea of a static training ship. Instead, they would assist other maritime organisations, and

The officers, crew and The Marine Society boys aboard the *Port Jackson*. These illustrations were included in a booklet – *Our Heritage The Sea* – which was intended to awaken public interest in sea-training.

British public, who owes so much to the sailor, will only do its part by assisting the Marine Society to carry on the work. Financial support is what is needed, and unless this is forthcoming it is perfectly clear that the coming voyage of the *Port Jackson* will, so far as the Marine Society is concerned, be her last as an ocean training-ship for forecastle seamen. And

Alfred J. West, F.R.G.S.   "*Our Navy.*"
"PORT JACKSON." OFFICERS, CREW, AND BOYS.

if this comes to pass one may almost be pardoned for assuming that they who "live at home at ease" care but little about the British mercantile marine, or whether it is manned by Britishers, or Dutchmen, or Dagoes. Public support is what is required. Shall it be said that this patriotic support is lacking? Surely not.

Doubtless there are some who will ask why, in this age of steamships, it is necessary for young sailors to be trained in sailing vessels. That it is necessary the seaman himself will be the first to admit. In a sailing ship a lad acquires that nerve and resourcefulness which have ever characterised the British seaman. The sail-trained man rises to an emergency better

Alfred J. West, F.R.G.S.   "*Our Navy.*"
"PORT JACKSON." GOOD-BYE.

than the steamboat man. By the period spent on the wind-jammer he becomes a sailor. He learns the value of discipline, and knows more of the "mystery of the sea" than had he gone first afloat on a big steam cargo-carrier. In earlier days the coasting brigs and schooners, the sailing fishing craft, and the speedy fruit-boats were an admirable school for train-

help individuals who wished to go to sea professionally but were unable to find the outlay necessary for their books, uniforms and other kit, amounting to between £60 and £80 for the average cadet or apprentice in 1949 (when its Secretary, Captain Lenny, retired after 31 years' service). The Society also helped the diversification of Lawrence Holt's Aberdovey Sea School, which had been founded in the war to improve the small-boat skills of the crews of Blue Funnel liners and enhance their chances of survival if their ships were sunk. Lawrence Holt and Otto Hahn, the exiled German educationalist and headmaster of Gordonstoun School, joined forces to establish the Outward Bound movement, attracting young men sponsored by industry for leadership and character assessment under harsh conditions. In 1949 The Marine Society, with the valuable *Ernest* in mind, provided funds to replace the school's ageing *Garibaldi* with an 80-ton training ketch, the 1891-built *Genesta*, renamed *Warspite*. Her master was for some time Alan Villiers, who later took the replica *Mayflower* across the Atlantic with a library on board provided by the SES.

The Outward Bound movement prospered in the brave new post-war world. In 1951, the former German pilot-vessel *Bremen*, later a fishermen's mission ship and latterly named *Prince Louis*, was bought by The Marine Society from Gordonstoun School and chartered for a peppercorn fee to the Moray Outward Bound Sea School at Burghead. Meanwhile, silting in the Dovey estuary meant that *Warspite* was too deep-draughted and in 1953 she was withdrawn, her station later taken by the *Golden Valley*. By the end of 1954 the *Prince Louis* had reached the end of her useful life and was replaced by a vessel of the same name. She had been built in 1878 and was disposed of later by the Society.

Meanwhile, the Seafarers' Education Service moved to larger premises at 207 Balham High Road. In 1947 it had acquired an ambitious new director in Dr Ronald Hope. While Mansbridge, with his penchant for reading westerns, was not himself an educated man and had been encouraged and supported by the Establishment because he was not a left-winger, his successor was both. Born in Battersea in 1921, the son of an unemployed ex-soldier, Hope followed his father into the Communist Party and remained a member until the Soviet Union attacked Finland. He attended Henry Thornton School at Clapham, where he was one of fifty British boys offered a trip to Canada funded by a wealthy industrialist. The party sailed westwards in the RMS *Ascania*, and six weeks later came home aboard the *Aurania*. This was Hope's first encounter with the British merchant navy, and back at school he became the corresponding member with the Shaw Savill and Albion liner *Ceramic* under the auspices of the British Ship Adoption Society, and in 1938 appeared on an early television broadcast with the *Ceramic*'s master, Captain H. C. Elphard.

Later the same year, Hope won an open exhibition in economics to New College, Oxford; going up a year later he gained a degree with First class honours. In 1941, he was called up and joined the Royal Navy as an Ordinary Seaman. Despite being earmarked for a commission, Hope's principles led to several confrontations with naval authority. In the first of these

The Society's second *Warspite* at her moorings, rigged with smaller spars than when in naval service. The boys nevertheless routinely set and furled sail as part of their pre-sea service training.

he led 800 Hostilities Only trainee ratings in a refusal to eat a breakfast of 'quite inedible kippers. The only reason my CW papers were not revoked was because no-one found out who organised the protest.' Hope was eventually commissioned as sub-lieutenant RNVR, passing out of HMS *Royal Alfred* at Lancing College top of his group. Shortly afterwards he underwent training as a Fighter Direction Officer and was then sent to America to await the completion of the escort-carrier HMS *Searcher*. After seeing active service in her, Hope served in a second carrier, HMS *Premier*, before transferring to the aircraft-directing ship HMS *Boxer*, in which he saw the end of the war 'abeam the casbah at Algiers on our way to the Far East'.

By September 1945 a request from New College found him back among the dreaming spires that he loved. Teaching economics part-time, he studied for his doctorate but, having married, he sought more active and remunerative employment than that of an Oxford academic. 'I was never very donnish,' he admits, 'but I was interested in adult education' and in 1947 he responded to an advertisement for Director of the Seafarers' Education Service.

He was exactly the right man for the job: young and energetic, with a quiet zeal for his task, Hope possessed an ease of manner that enabled him to persuade a shipping magnate to fund the SES as sensitively as he could induce a ship's cook to undertake a course in English literature. This he combined with a formidable intellect, also persuading a wide range of honorary tutors to take on students from what many had once considered an improbable source. Such enviable qualities endeared him to many in the wide world of British shipping, and numerous and varied were those who were honoured to call him friend. Hope was, by any standards, an extraordinary man: a convinced atheist with that respect for men and women from vastly different backgrounds, he lived by the tenets of a robust socialism and was happiest when encouraging a seafarer in some academic quest. Even those who never took up a correspondence course with the College of the Sea, which, apart from a small nominal payment to cover postage, was otherwise free of charge, benefited from the ship's libraries which were carefully chosen to reflect a wide range of interest.

Ronald Hope, former Director of the Seafarers' Education Service, seen here enjoying his retirement in Scotland, 2004.

A *WARSPITE* BOY 1936-1937

Philip Okill

"I hated school and told my father I wanted to go to sea. He was a local government officer and we lived in respectable, middle-class Sevenoaks. My father brought the prospectuses of the three Thames training ships home and asked which one I wanted to join. Of the *Worcester*, *Exmouth* and *Warspite* I chose the last named, not knowing that the *Worcester* was the officer-cadets, ship and the *Warspite* was for orphans. I insisted on her because, unlike the others which were old wooden-walls, *Warspite* was 'a Third Class Armoured Cruiser of the Great War', a highly seductive description.

In a dingy office in Bishopsgate my eyes were tested by an ex-RN petty officer; after which I was accepted. Being financially secure, my father was expected to make a contribution which he did, I think, to teach me a lesson but my first acquaintance with the ship was a shock. We slept in hammocks out of which we were turned at 0530 every morning to take a cold shower. Sluggards were hastened along by one of the ship's retired naval petty officers who wielded a 'stonnicky', or persuader.

The food was adequate, but monotonous, the cook was thought to be mad and if one was assigned duty to help in the galley one had to be aware of his frequent outburst of temper which might result in a large pot of soup being hurled to the deck, only to be cleaned up by the cook's boy.

We had plenty of activities, swimming, boxing, cross-country running and, of course, boat-work, parades and inspections. If you were any good at pursing your lips and getting a noise out of a bugle, you could find yourself in the ship's band. We became competent at pulling a boat and took part in regattas with the other training ships. On the academic side, in addition to nautical studies, which included all the then customary skills such as knots and splices, boxing the compass, the Rule of the Road, and so on, our general education was up to matriculation standard. Supervising this we had an Education Officer who served under the Captain-Superintendent who lived aft in the former captain's quarters. The petty-officer instructors lived ashore, though they slept aboard during their duty watches. Another daily attendee was our nurse and if we fell ill, there was a sickbay ashore. We were also regularly visited by the Padre, who was a fine chap.

I got on well with the other lads and our dissimilar backgrounds were not a problem. I was lucky enough to hit the ship's bully hard enough in the boxing ring to wind him and he never afterwards picked on me while it made me popular with the other boys. Of course, we were all in uniform and all lived under the same regime, so there were no differences. This produced good camaraderie and we learned to stand up for ourselves and while things were tough, there was never any cruelty and for the most part everyone was very decent.

I could take the rough life but I learned that if I was intent on a career in the Royal Navy I would have to spend two years in *Warspite* and then go on to a proper naval training 'ship', either of the 'stone frigates' HMS *Ganges*, near Harwich, or HMS *St Vincent*, near Portsmouth. I didn't fancy this much, but I learned that if I opted for the merchant service I could leave and go to sea after six months, so I chose this course of action. Moored as we were off Grays, we were constantly watching the ships and sailing-barges going up and down the river, so the attraction of being on one of those ships was strong. In 1937 I signed on as a bridge-boy aboard the trans-Atlantic liner *Berengaria*. Mind you, it was out of the frying pan into the fire, because my bunk in this crack ship was full of bed-bugs and the chief officer turned out to like boys, but the *Warspite* had toughened me for that sort of thing and I called him a 'dirty bastard', after which he left me alone.

After a couple of years at sea, I looked up from working in the holds one day and saw a young chap in uniform elegantly smoking a cigarette as he leaned over the rail of the bridge and I thought, I want to be up there, not down here. I didn't have any trouble with sitting my Second Mate's examination and, as by this time war had broken out the Board of Trade were not very strict on sea-time. So I became an officer and I suppose justified my father's ultimate faith in me."

We slept in hammocks out of which we were turned at 0530 every morning to take a cold shower.

The Seafarers' Education Service and College of the Sea, with its crest of an heraldic 'sea-dog' bearing a torch of learning, entered a period of dynamic achievement. Countless seafarers strove to improve themselves much as Mansbridge had foreseen, many obtaining degrees or other qualifications. Since 1934 the SES had issued a quarterly journal, *The Seafarer*, which not only provided a platform for poetry, short stories and competitions for literary and artistic prizes, but also disseminated information about seafarers' achievements among a wider public ashore. One English tutor, Jean Crowcroft, recalled that in becoming a voluntary tutor she 'had the pleasure not only of helping students develop their powers of expression but also of improving my own. That seafarers seem to take a particular interest in language is evident in the quality of the poems I have encountered as judge of the annual competition, and one more reason why it has been a privilege to participate in the activities of the Society.'

In 1954 the Seafarers' Education Service and College of the Sea were incorporated by Royal Charter and that same year Hope initiated a film library so that merchant seafarers

View from the bridge of a Royal Fleet Auxiliary tanker.

could watch films at sea. He fostered his students, bringing some ashore to help the work of the SES. He also assigned tutors to ships, to encourage the on-board study and practice of the arts, mathematics and physical education. The first sea-going tutor was the artist Grenville Cottingham, and a later one was the composer John Hawkins, who subsequently composed a Sea Symphony.

In the post-war period the British merchant navy enjoyed a boom, and The Marine Society became largely concerned with finding bursaries for young men bent on going to sea. In 1957 The Marine Society Act was passed to amend the Society's powers of investment, and two years later it rebuilt its offices to secure a better return. That year the Sailors' Home and Red Ensign Club between Dock and Ensign Streets was also rebuilt. In 1962 Ronald Hope joined the Committee of The Marine Society and in 1964, on the retirement of Commander Richard Burgess, a new secretary was appointed. This was Captain Charles Wickham Malins DSO DSC* RN, a tall and distinguished former destroyer officer whose last appointment had been Director of the Admiralty Trade Division, a post that had familiarised him with the customs and practices of shipping companies and the nature of merchant naval officers. 'Ticky' Malins did not consider the position of Secretary of the Society as a post-retirement sinecure. He shared Hope's vision of making something more of The Marine Society and of creating a proper professional body for the merchant navy. He found the Society's activities 'satisfactory enough, but … to some extent out of date; charities need to keep up with the times and … The Marine Society needed a more positive role.' Hope was more forthright, convinced that The Marine Society had lost much of its sense of purpose.

Acutely aware that the Royal Navy had in some respects usurped the prime position of the merchant marine as the chief source of maritime power, Hope and Malins were determined to enhance the status of merchant seafarers generally and of the officers in particular. The merchant fleet was, after all, a wealth creating sea-service which in wartime both augmented the Royal Navy and provided the fourth arm of national defence. In this there were echoes of Hanway's original purpose brought up to date. Malins wanted to foster a body which enhanced and protected the professionalism of merchant naval masters and officers,

A ship's library from The Marine Society.

an institute distinct from any trade union and inclusive of the corps as a whole. Hope supported this notion, considering a union-based ethos as unlikely to attract the respect the calling ought to have. Naturally the Merchant Navy and Airline Officers' Association, the representative trade union, was opposed to the establishment of any such entity, as were the ship-owners who saw, looming in raised status, the spectre of higher salaries. Nevertheless, with the help of Trinity House and the leadership of its Deputy Master, Sir George Barnard, a trust was established to promote the idea and raise money, to which The Marine Society contributed the hefty sum of £5,000. Having applied for incorporation under the Companies Act, the Nautical Institute was launched in 1971 at The Marine Society's Hanway House, Bishopsgate, though it later moved along the street to Alderman's House. As part of their joint initiative, Malins and Hope made a major contribution to the formation of the Nautical Institute, recommending a former College of the Sea student and Blue Funnel officer, Julian Parker, as its first Secretary.

Sadly, the birth of this now international institute was set against a sombre background: the British merchant navy was beginning a long decline. By 1966, the numbers of new entrants was falling and in any case the condition of the last ratings' training ship, the *Vindicatrix* at Sheerness, was so poor that she had to be sold. Her would-be seamen and stewards were taken in by the National Sea Training School at Gravesend which, as HMS *Worcester*, was rebuilt, raised to 'college' status and began to run courses for all ranks. This assumption of an old name was due to the *Worcester* herself closing in 1968 through a lack of cadets.

Although The General Council of British Shipping inaugurated a British Shipping Careers Service, a period of extensive reorganisation followed as nautical charities found themselves adrift. Too many disparate bodies were providing services for the merchant navy, most of them charities with limited and specific purposes. Some, like the Ship Adoption Society and the Red Ensign Club in Dock Street, were in financial difficulties while others such as the Merchant Navy Comforts Service were no longer required. The Society had already dealt with one redundant body, the old Naval Officers' Widows' Fund, winding it up and transferring its funds to The Officers' Association.

FIFTY POUNDS AND OFF TO SEA

"I was born and brought up in a small market gardening town in Worcestershire. We weren't poor but we were six kids so money wasn't easy to find for us, and I did odd jobs in cafes and on the land, where there was casual work for a 12-year-old. I was in trouble at grammar school in 1968, when I was just turning 16, and doing O-levels. I just wanted to get away from school and home, so I decided to go to sea. I don't remember how I found out vacancies, but there was a shortage of applicants in those days for apprenticeships, which were just becoming cadetships. I applied to Cayzer Irvine, and was accepted. I was told I had to go to the School of Navigation at Warsash for a year's pre-sea training where I was one of the first company-funded cadets sent there.

Warsash sent me a whacking great kit list, full of stiff and semi-stiff collars, tropical whites and buckskin shoes, all sorts of thing which I'd never heard of. I didn't even have a pair of pyjamas. All this cost about £150 and although my parents were happy that I wanted to go to sea, they took no interest and couldn't give me any cash. I worked all I could, after school and at weekends, but at one shilling per hour it was a long haul. Somehow I found out about The Marine Society and they gave me £50 to help. So that's how they got me into Warsash and off to sea.

Once at sea I realised that I had been a fool to ignore languages at school, so I used the SES to set me up with tutors to learn languages. I learnt Greek and Spanish, and subsequently married a Spanish girl, although I can't blame the SES for that. I studied other subjects and devoured the books in the ships' libraries, asking for special books, which I always got. Then I began to enter their writing competitions, and with Dr Hope's encouragement, had a few short stories and poems published in *The Seafarer*, and in a couple of the anthologies Dr Hope published.

All this time I was steadily getting my tickets, and eventually went up for Extra Master in 1980. While doing that I got annoyed by a salesman from Sperry who was snotty to me when I pointed out that his new CAS radar, the first of its type, was duff. So I wrote a piece for *Fairplay* spoofing the radar. It was published, I got paid £50, and that began a four or five year period on which I wrote as a paid hobby for all the shipping press. I was working as the Principal Ship Surveyor for the Dept of Transport in South Africa by then, having sailed as Mate for seven years and seen the UK fleet collapsing around my ears. With two young kids, an insistent wife and a good salary, what else can an Extra Master do?

My wife was unhappy in South Africa and wanted to be back in Europe, and just by coincidence as my contract was coming to an end, Mike Grey left *Fairplay*. I had been writing for *Fairplay* regularly for some time, and so I asked about joining them. I was hired as deputy editor in 1988, and stayed there until 1995. I wrote two books during that time, both still in print. *Marine Surveying and Consultancy* is the standard text book, and *Effective Writing for the Marine Industry* is a steady seller. Then I left, with some other staff, and we founded Merlin. Today Merlin is the largest maritime public relations company in the world, with clients in every maritime field; we also own a maritime magazine publishing company. I've built up a couple of parallel careers, first as an expert witness, then as an arbitrator, and as a trainer and I currently get quite a lot of work as a paid chairman and moderator of conferences and seminars. Funnily enough, I get hired to teach effective writing to professionals, such as lawyers.

If you'd asked me at any stage of that what I was going to do next, I'd never have guessed, but I always had a debt of gratitude to Dr Hope and The Marine Society."

John Guy

Somehow I found out about The Marine Society and they gave me £50 to help...

In 1972 *Worcester*'s parent body, the Incorporated Thames Nautical Training College, was liquidated and the freehold of its Ingress Abbey Estate at Greenhithe passed to the Seafarers' Education Service. On the closure of HMS *Worcester* the site had been let to the Inner London Education Authority, who had optimistically established the new Merchant Navy College on the site but, as the British merchant fleet shrank, the college was to be short lived, and closed in 1986. Artefacts from the *Worcester* were sold to provide a scholarship fund for higher academic and professional advancement. The 120-year lease on the estate was surrendered and the Marine Society began a prolonged process of divesting itself of the property, which included the dilapidated but Grade II-listed abbey itself. Shortly after acquiring the freehold, the Seafarers' Education Service absorbed the ailing British Ship Adoption Society while at the same time, The Marine Society became trustees for The Destitute Sailors' Fund and took over the Sailors' Home and Red Ensign Club, including the London School of Nautical Cookery.

In 1976, under an approved Charity Commission Scheme and an Order in Council, the Seafarers' Education Service merged with The Marine Society; Hope became the new Director with Malins remaining as Secretary. The new organisation, which retained the older title of The Marine Society but was thereafter governed by a Council, absorbed the residual funds of the Merchant Navy Comforts Service Trust. With the Marine Society in Clark's Place, Bishopsgate, the Nautical Institute nearby, and the Seafarers' Education Service occupying Mansbridge House in Balham, there was a need for centralised premises. Malins and Hope set about finding a suitable property.

Studying on board with the College of the Sea.

A super-tanker at sea by Peter Knox, one of the Society's artist tutors.

> One afternoon [Malins recalled], Hope and I happily found a vacant Church of England Boy's School overlooking Archbishop's Park in Lambeth. The school had been closed some four years before, the pupils having been transferred to a nearby comprehensive leaving a substantial Edwardian school building complete with a playground and gatehouse to the mercy of vandals who had done their worst. Purchasing this derelict property … did not prove all that straightforward, for the

Storm Petrel — Peter Knox

Church Authorities who were prepared to sell … for quite a modest sum … could not prove their title to the freehold. The trouble had arisen when the school was built in 1904 by the then Archbishop of Canterbury, William Temple, who had said airily, "Take a bit of my park," and so they did, forgetting … any legal formality. In the end the Charity Commissioners again came to our aid declaring that, as the school had squatted on a corner of the Archbishop's Park for some seventy years, the governors could be deemed to own the property and thus … sell it.

Repairs and alterations to the new headquarters were 'extensive and costly' but on completion the buildings proved effective and, as it transpired, adaptable. 'The old assembly hall became our library housing many thousands of books for making up into ship's libraries, with the cookery school housed on a new floor overhead. There were, moreover, a number of self-catering study bedrooms in the former headmaster's house over the gateway.' Happily, the old school also provided a headquarters for the Nautical Institute and a London office for the RNLI. On the completion of the refurbishment, the splendid neo-gothic complex was formally opened in 1979. In pouring rain, Her Majesty The Queen unveiled a sundial which combined the armillary sphere of The Nautical Institute with the sea-dog The Marine Society had adopted from the Seafarers' Education Service and College of the Sea.

The enhanced Marine Society continued to provide and develop educational services to the mariner, along with the provision of libraries to merchant ships. A wider pastoral care was offered too by the additional provision of tutors and fitness instructors as well as model kits and film libraries. Encouragement, direction and financial support, including interest-free loans, continued to be given to promising seafarers anxious to enhance their qualifications, and remained an important part of the Society's work. Liaison with schools also continued in the programme of the Sea Lines, as the Ship Adoption scheme had been renamed to enable children to continue to take an interest in the maritime world and opening the prospect of a career at sea to those so minded.

Alas, the pall of gloom over British shipping was growing as ship-owners continued to

An entry into The Marine Society's annual art competition for seafarers – 'Ship's Postman'.

sell ships or flag them out in order to benefit from cheap Third World labour. Unfortunately, this coincided with the introduction of larger tankers and containerisation, which alone increased the capacity of individual ships and reduced the number of bottoms required. Such modern vessels incorporated automated systems and an increasing array of electronic equipment, factors which still further reduced the size of each ship's crew. Consequently the British rating faced extinction while the British officer, on deck or in the engine room, was often driven to seek employment abroad or under flags of convenience, a fact marked in 1982 by the termination of the British Shipping Careers Service.

By the early 1980s the funds of the Society were beginning to benefit from the sale of Clark's Place in Bishopsgate and the properties at Balham, the former Mercantile Marine Office in Ensign Street and its neighbour in Dock Street. The proceeds had been wisely invested to generate an increasing income which allowed the Council to support with significant grants the Sea Cadet Corps and other maritime youth organisations, including the *Foudroyant*. As mentioned earlier, she was a half-sister to the Society's own *Venus* and had lain at her moorings in Portsmouth harbour for many years as a static training ship for school and youth groups whose members might follow a career at sea. The old frigate had been acquired in 1892 by the philanthropist Wheatley Cobb to replace an earlier *Foudroyant* which had flown Nelson's flag in 1799 and had in turn been named after a French ship captured in 1758. Cobb's original *Foudroyant* was towed round the coast as a project designed to give eager boys a whiff of the briny and a glimpse of life at sea, but she was driven ashore by a gale when anchored off Blackpool in June 1897 and became a total loss. In 1905 Cobb acquired the *Trincomalee* which he renamed *Foudroyant*; originally moored in Falmouth, in 1932 she was moved to Portsmouth Harbour. The Marine Society made several grants of up to £3 million to sustain the old ship but by 1982 she too had been closed down, to be taken to Hartlepool where she has since been splendidly restored and today lies open to visitors.

The Society continued to encourage maritime activities among young people to whom a sea-going career might appeal. The modern world has learned, contrary to Hanway's confident expectations, that society's 'progress' is not axiomatic; more comfortable living

Another art competition picture – 'Painting a mast'.
Able seamen aloft on a British merchant ship.
R. Lamb.

conditions, increased leisure and disposable income introduce temptation. Ever-relaxing attitudes towards sexual freedom, drugs and 'youth-culture' provide added stimuli to anti-social behaviour, while globalisation and the free market have destroyed socialism and the Utopian dream. A universal mercantilism has largely abandoned its Christian virtues and the young are profoundly affected. As Britain lost her industrial base and painfully reinvented herself, the Marine Adventure Sailing Trust was set up by the then Treasurer, Richard Thornton, to raise income, administered by The Marine Society, for the encouragement and support of maritime youth organisations, especially the *Foudroyant* and the Sea Cadet brig *Royalist*. Described by council members as 'an imaginative and successful scheme', the trust was Thornton's inspiration. The Society subscribed loan capital of £300,000 to a split capital trust with total assets of £1,050,000. Although the Society waived any gain on capital investment, it enjoyed all the income earned by the trust during its short life and by this means was enabled to increase its donations to sail-training.

Meanwhile, in the wider merchant service, as falling crew numbers were irrevocably changing the nature of seafaring, the Society also consolidated its activities, ending its model kits and film library services. In 1986, the cookery school at Lambeth was closed and transferred to the National Sea Training College at Gravesend. That year also saw the closure of the Dreadnought Seaman's Hospital at Greenwich which, like The Marine Society, had once housed its wards in an old hulk moored in London's river.

Despite these contractions, it was not all bad news, for in 1984 the Society's council had taken the decision to renew its support for specific sea-training, and the first course was run aboard the *Resolute of Thames*, a 40-feet yacht loaned by her owner, Richard Thornton. The following year a modification to the Charity Order amended the Society's powers of fiscal management and investment and, having run a second successful sea-training course in the *Halcyon*, a large 69-feet ketch which had been the cadet-training vessel belonging to the former Warsash School of Navigation, the council decided to acquire its own motor-driven training vessel.

This was achieved in 1986, the year Ronald Hope retired and Lieutenant Commander

Anchorwork aboard the training ship *Earl of Romney*.

The Marine Society's two training ships *Jonas Hanway* and *Earl of Romney* in Ramsgate, *c*.1995.

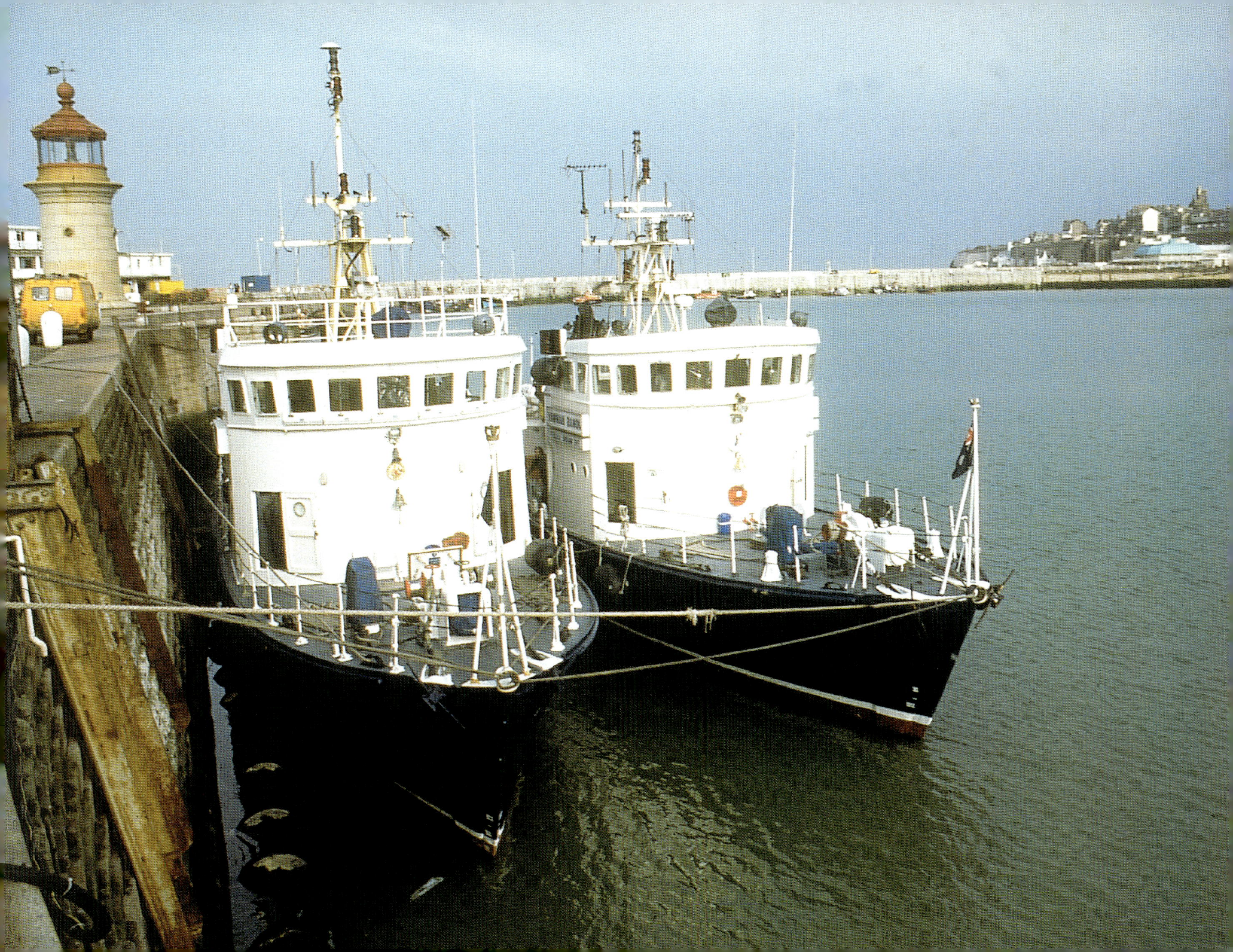

Richard Frampton RN relieved him as Director. Frampton's connection with the Society had begun in 1980 when he had relieved Malins as Secretary, and he now combined both offices, becoming the Society's General Secretary. After a trawl through the sale list of some 130 vessels, none of which seemed suitable, the then Director of the Naval Education Service suggested that the Society should consider asking the Royal Navy for the loan of HMS *Egeria*, a modified, 1959-built inshore hydrographic survey vessel. Refitting for training purposes was undertaken at Dartmouth by Phillip & Son. On 10 December 1986, the bicentenary of the commissioning of the *Beatty* as *The Marine Society*, the *Egeria* was renamed *Jonas Hanway* by Mrs Margaret Watts, a vice-president of the Society, former chairman of The Merchant Navy Comforts Service, member of an old ship-owning family and whose husband, Edmund Watts, had been the founder of the Ship Adoption Society.

The *Jonas Hanway* immediately began operations from Gravesend, where her home mooring lay off the National Sea Training College, the school for trainee ratings for the merchant navy. The take-up of places was encouraging and within three months the Society decided to purchase her sister-ships, *Echo* and *Enterprise*. The *Enterprise* was to be stripped for spares and eventually sold as a bare hulk but the *Echo* enjoyed a new lease of life. After refitting at Hebburn on Tyneside she was handed over to the Society on 1 June 1988. At the end of that month she was renamed the *Earl of Romney* at Tower Pier, London, by Mrs Julian Marsham, wife of the heir to the then Earl of Romney.

With a length of 32.5 metres, beam of 6.5 metres and a draught of just over 2 metres these two small diesel-powered, 10-knot vessels of 189 tons displacement proved ideal for their purpose. They became well known in home and near-Continental waters, operating year round from Gravesend and providing a training opportunity to many young people from all walks of life and all parts of the country. Groups of up to a dozen trainees of both sexes and over 12 years of age accompanied by two adult instructors embarked for periods extending from a weekend to a full week; many youth groups made the trip annually. The Marine Society's smart little ships had a standing staff of master, mate, two engineers and a cook, all of whom were drawn from three rostered groups under Captains Michael Mills,

Sea Cadets on board the *Earl of Romney*.

***Jonas Hanway* at sea.**

Christopher Roberts and Graham Smith. But it was the enthusiastic youngsters whose part in running the ships was vital both to the safe conduct of the vessels themselves and to their own training, that made up the crews on voyages which extended from the estuaries of the Thames and Medway to France, Belgium and down Channel. On the closure of the National Sea Training School at Gravesend in the winter of 1998, both vessels were obliged to shift their base to the Medway. Here new moorings were taken up off the Chatham Historic Dockyard, where Hanway's brother Thomas had once been the commissioner.

From 1986 the Society had been able to fund not only the Seafarers' Libraries, the College of the Sea, Sea Lines, sea-going tutors and the two training ships, but also to cover the costs of preparing the 35-acre Ingress Abbey Estate for sale at a reasonable price and show a surplus. However, a subsequent downturn in the property market and the resulting long and expensive planning applications took their toll of income. As if this were not enough, investment income was affected by volatility on the stock market and the withdrawal of the tax credits on dividends. By 1997, with no income improvement in sight and a steady continuing erosion of the Society's capital, the Council reluctantly decided that the *Jonas Hanway* must be returned to the Royal Navy, thus cutting some of the deficit. However, the position eased a little when Ingress Abbey was finally sold to a property developer the following year.

Nevertheless, the *Earl of Romney* continued the good work, operating from Chatham from autumn to spring and venturing to Southampton and the Channel Island ports in the summer. Although she had a life expectancy of a further eight years, the prolonged drain on funds worried the council and the decision was taken to decommission the vessel at the end of 2004. Together, the *Jonas Hanway* and the *Earl of Romney* had taken 23,300 trainees, among whom could be numbered prospective seafarers such as naval reservists and potential naval officer candidates, together with corporate groups and youth organisations like the Sea Cadets, Sea Scouts, Air Cadets, school parties and youth clubs.

However, the Society's active involvement in sea-training for the young did not end there. The facilities provided by the *Jonas Hanway* and *Earl of Romney* had long since created a symbiosis between the Society and the Sea Cadets. The Sea Cadet Corps' origins date back to

A ship's master visiting a primary school to inspire the next generation of potential seafarers.

Metamorphoses and initiatives

the Boys' Naval Brigade, founded in the early twentieth century by the Navy League, jointly sponsored by the Admiralty and later, the Ministry of Defence (Navy). In 1976 the Navy League was renamed the Sea Cadet Association, which continued to administer and (with the Royal Navy) sponsor the corps. In 1987 its headquarters had moved into The Marine Society's domain at 202 Lambeth Road and by the millennium, four hundred Sea Cadet units (including one in Malta) had trained almost 15,000 young people, both boys and girls, and similar corps existed elsewhere in the Commonwealth. Central to the Sea Cadets' training are the 29-metre steel-hulled brig *Royalist*, built in 1972, and the 24-metre grp motor vessel *John Jerwood*, which entered service in 2002. Both vessels are based in Gosport, from where they provide facilities to train aspirants in leadership and seamanship skills, including a syllabus which can lead to the acquisition of Royal Yachting Association qualifications.

On the disposal of *Earl of Romney*, The Marine Society's governing council had resolved not to abandon practical sea-training, and the contiguity of both The Marine Society's premises and its purpose led to an inevitable conjunction with the Sea Cadet Association. The Marine Society has evolved by a policy of harnessing the winds of change for its charitable aims, most recently in its successful combination with the Seafarers' Education Service. The

A Merchant Navy cadet on watch on the bridge of his ship.

Sea Cadets at the International Festival of the Sea, Portsmouth, 2005.

HMS *Chatham*, a Royal Navy Type 22 frigate.

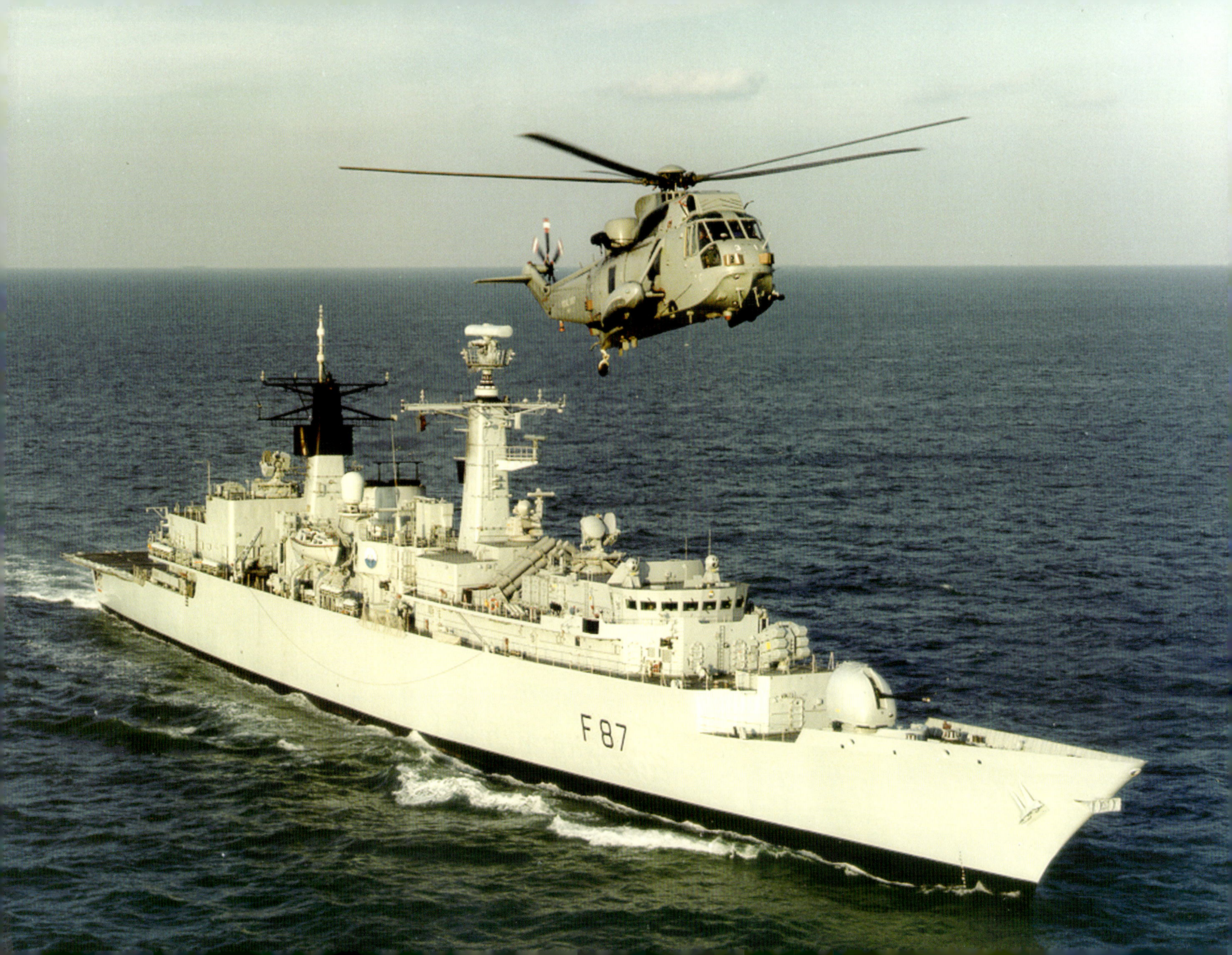
F 87

proposed union with the Sea Cadet Association was but a further step in this evolutionary chain. As Patron of both The Marine Society and The Sea Cadet Association, Her Majesty The Queen graciously consented to continue as Patron of the merged charities, which were henceforth to be known as 'The Marine Society and Sea Cadets'. After approval from the Charity Commission the merger was effected on 30 November 2004 and Captain Jeremy Howard RN, the Society's final Director – the title having been revived upon his appointment in February 1997 – handed over to Michael Cornish who, as Chief Executive of the Sea Cadet Association, now assumed the new office of Chief Executive of The Marine Society and Sea Cadets.

The Marine Society remains committed to supporting the education, training and well-being of its predominantly merchant naval beneficiaries through the College of the Sea, the library service, financial assistance and careers advice. These objectives will remain as long

The Marine Society and Sea Cadets training brig *Royalist* begins another Tall Ships Race.

as a demand among British seafarers is sustained. But there is a decline in the numbers of young people seeking careers at sea, fed in part by an increasing national indifference to, or ignorance of, our reliance upon sea-borne trade for our well-being. This has created a situation in which a short-fall of people suitable to support the marine infrastructure – from ship-brokers and insurers, to assessors, surveyors, pilots, harbour-masters and port-staff such as traffic control officers – is becoming increasingly apparent. Ironically, it is a situation that Hanway and his friends would have been only too familiar with two hundred and fifty years ago, and the Society's council recognised the importance of addressing it. The Marine Society therefore lent its support to the Sea Vision UK campaign initiated by The Chamber of Shipping – the association of British ship-owners – which is aimed at rekindling public interest in the national importance of the marine industries, including seafaring itself.

By these metamorphoses and initiatives, a continuity of intent has been, and is being, maintained, with the Sea Cadet vessels carrying on the work of the *Jonas Hanway* and the *Earl of Romney*. Thus, in an ever-changing world, charity and policy have again achieved another pragmatic union.

Britain's maritime prognosis is uncertain, though London continues to be an important centre of shipping business. Government policy, initiated by a former College of the Sea student, Deputy Prime Minister John Prescott, seeks to attract ships to the British ensign with a favourable tax regime. In 2006, at the time of The Marine Society's 250th Anniversary, one thing remains certain: whatever the future, Britain's prosperity depends upon over nine-tenths of her imports and exports moving safely by sea. Much of this trade is, and always has been, carried in foreign vessels; but Britain has always required seafarers to serve and service her maritime needs, people like those boys of daring temper first recruited for the sea-service in 1756 by Hanway and his colleagues. With these aims in mind, The Marine Society and Sea Cadets remains dedicated to supporting that essential requirement, howsoever the shifting sands of circumstance dictate.

OFFICERS OF THE MARINE SOCIETY

1756-2006

PRESIDENTS

1772	Robert, 2nd Baron of Romney (*mentioned in the Act of Incorporation*)
1793	Charles, 1st Earl of Romney
1811	Charles, 2nd Earl of Romney
1845	Charles, 3rd Earl of Romney
1874	Charles, 4th Earl of Romney
1905	Charles, 5th Earl of Romney
1933	Charles, 6th Earl of Romney
1974	The Viscount Runciman of Doxford, OBE, AFC
1989	Michael, 7th Earl of Romney
2004-	Admiral Sir Peter Abbott, GBE, KCB

TREASURERS

1756	John Thornton, Esq.
1783	Samuel Thornton, Esq., MP
1831	William Thornton Astell, Esq., MP
1847	Henry Sykes Thornton, Esq.
1882	Edward Thornton, Esq., CB
1888	John Francis William Deacon, Esq.
1941	Lieutenant-Colonel the Hon. Ian Leslie Melville, TD
1954	Christopher E. Thornton, Esq.
1980	Richard C. Thornton, Esq.
1992	Christopher C. Thornton, Esq.
2003-2004	Henry D. C. Thornton, Esq.

SECRETARIES

1756	John Stephens
1762	John Bowdridge-Webb
1762	N. Gilchrist
1764–1769	Unknown
1769	C. Launder
1770	Thomas Myers
1770	Thomas Birch
1770	Charles Sulsh
1774	Joshua Cowell
1775	Thomas Knowles Gosnell
1777	James Hailes
1778	Thomas Burford
1778	William May
1778	Thomas Ramsey
1780	Thomas Vowell
1782	John Newby
1821	Thomas King (*Assistant Secretary from 1801*)
1868	S. Whitchurch Sadler, Paymaster-in-Chief, RN
1884	Henry W. Andrews, Fleet Paymaster, RN (*Assistant Secretary from 1877*)
1892	Lieutenant Albert Edwin Poland, RN
1900-1918	Commander Henry T. A. Bosanquet, RN
1914	David W. Carr, Esq. (*pro tem*)
1915	Thomas Sedwick, Esq. (*pro tem*)
1919	Captain Charles G. A. Lenny, RN
1949	Commander C. R. Burgess, OBE, RN
1964	Captain C. W. Malins, DSO, DSC*, RN
1980	Lieutenant Commander R. M. Frampton, RN

GENERAL SECRETARY

1986-1994	Lieutenant Commander R. M. Frampton, RN

DIRECTORS

1976-1986	Dr R. S. Hope, CBE
1994-1996	Lieutenant Commander R.M. Frampton, RN
1997-2004	Captain J. J. Howard, MBE, RN

CHIEF EXECUTIVE OFFICER
(The Marine Society and Sea Cadets)

2004-	M. J. Cornish, Esq.

INDEX OF NAMES

Including individuals, organisations and vessels, but excluding The Marine Society, the Royal Navy and the Merchant Navy or associated forms.

Aberdovey Sea School 98
Admiralty 10, 14, 19, 24, 44, 49, 50, 58, 67, 75, 76, 103, 114
Aeneas, SS 94
Agamemnon, HMS 41-42
Air Cadets 113
Akbar 60
Alfred Holt & Company 63, 94, 98
Anson, Lord 22
Arethusa, HMS 48, 60, 78
Arnold, William 41
Ascania, RMS 99
Aurania, RMS 99

Barfleur, HMS 19
Barnard, Sir George 104
Bates, Thomas 41
Bayley, Commander L. H. 81, 87
Beale, Dr 72
Beatty 38, 40, 48, 49, 112
Beef-Steake Society, Gentlemen of the 22
Beresford, Lord 76
Bethel, The Right Honourable Slingsby 2
Blackmore, Captain Edward 60
Blackwood, Captain Henry 69
Blue Funnel Line 94, 98, 104
Board of Education 92
Board of Trade 58, 60, 71, 86
Board Schools 33
Bombay Marine 54
Boscawen, Admiral Lord 22
Boxer, HMS 100
Boy Scouts 89
Boys' Brigade 89
Boys' Naval Brigade 114
Brackenbury, Captain 74
Brassey, Lord 58, 59, 60, 62, 71, 76
Bremen, German pilot-vessel 98
British Sailors' Society 55

British Ship Adoption Society 96, 99, 104, 106, 108
British Shipping Careers Service 104, 109
Brown, Tom 26
Budgen, Frank 69
Burgess, Commander Richard 103

Calder, Sir Robert 49
Cambridge, Duke of 76
Carnegie UK Trust 94
Ceramic, SS 99
Chamber of Commerce 56
Chamber of Shipping 117
Charity Commission 106, 108, 116
Chichester, HMS 60
Christ's Hospital 20
Church Lads' Brigade 89
Clarence, HMS 60
Clio, HMS 67
Cobb, Wheatley 109
College of the Sea 95, 101, 102, 108, 116, 117
Conqueror, HMS, previously *Waterloo* 67
Conway, HMS 60
Cooke, Thomas Potter 42
Cornish, Michael J. 116
Cornwall, HMS 60
Cornwall, John 10
Cottingham, Grenville 103
County Naval Free Schools 36, 38
Cumberland, HMS 60
Cunard Line 75

Dame Schools 33
Destitute Sailors' Asylum (later, Rest) 55, 70, 78, 106
Devitt & Moore 71, 72, 74
Devitt, Philip 74-75
Devitt, Sir Thomas 71, 72
Dingley, Charles 9, 20
Dreadnought, HMS 76
Dreadnought Seaman's Hospital 110

Earl of Romney 112, 113, 114, 117
East India Company 52
Echo 112
Edinburgh, Duke of 76

Egeria, HMS 112
Ellerman Trust 94
Elliott, Rear-Admiral George 58
Elphard, Captain H. C. 99
Enterprise 112
Ernest, sailing tender 75, 88

F. T. Everard, ship-owners 80
Fielding, Henry 18
Fielding, Sir John 18-19, 20, 22, 24, 30, 33, 37
Fisher, Herbert 76
Fluyd, Mr 25, 26
Folkestone, Viscount 21
Formidable, HMS 34, 60
Foudroyant 109, 110
Foundling Hospital for Orphans 8, 9, 10, 19, 20
Frampton, Lt-Commander Richard M., RN 112
Franklin, John 25, 26
Furnell, Captain 59

Garibaldi 98
Garrick, David 21, 24
Genesta, mv 98
George II, HM King 21, 24
George III, HM King 33
George V, HM King 90
George, Prince of Wales 21
Gibraltar, HMS 60
Glasse, Reverend Samuel 34, 37
Glynn, Chief Instructor 72
Golden Valley 98
Goliath, HMS 60, 67, 78
Goodwin, Arthur 80-81
Gray, Thomas 62

HM Coastguard 55, 80
HM Customs and Excise 44
Hahn, Otto 98
Halcyon 110
Hall, Joseph 25
Hanway, Jonas 1-13, *passim* thereafter
Hanway, Thomas 19, 113
Harbinger, HMS 71
Hardy, Thomas Masterman 22

Harvey, Commander H. G. L. 81
Haskey, Henry, (Apothecary) 21, 25, 26, 32
Havannah, HMS 60
Hawke, Admiral Lord 22
Hawkins, John 103
Hermione, HMS 80, 86
Hesperus, HMS 71
Hickes, William 30, 32-33
Hill, Captain A. G. K., RN 80
Holmes, Walter 42
Holt, Lawrence 94, 98
Hood, HMS 96
Hope, Dr Ronald S., CBE 94, 95, 98-102, 104, 106, 110
Howard, Captain Jeremy J., MBE, RN 116

Illawarra, HMS 74
Impregnable, HMS 80
Impress Service 10, 16, 29
Indefatigable, HMS 60
'Independent Ships' 62
Industrial Schools 60
Inner London Education Authority 106
Iphigenia, HMS 54
Iris, HMS 49

James, John 21
Jervis Bay, HMS 96
John Jerwood, mv 114
Jonas Hanway, mv 112, 113, 117

King George's Fund for Sailors 77

Lenny, Captain Charles, RN 80, 98
Lind, Dr James 19
Livesay, G. H. P. 75
London Sailors' Home 71
London School of Nautical Cookery 71, 87, 106
Louis of Battenberg, Admiral Prince 76

Magdalen Hospital 8
Maitland, Captain Charles 74
Malins, Captain Charles Wickham (Ticky), DSO DSC RN 103-104, 106, 112
Manby, Captain 55
Mansbridge, Albert 90, 92, 94, 98, 102

Index

Marine Adventure Sailing Trust 110
Marine Society 40, 41, 44
Marine Society and Sea Cadets 116
Marine Society Fishing Company 44
Maritime School 34, 36, 37
Marryat, Frederick 36, 56,
Mars, HMS 60
Marsham, Robert (*see* Romney, Earl of)
Martin, James 42
Maude, steam-launch 70
Mead, Frederick 87
Mercantile Marine Office 56, 58, 109
Merchant Navy and Airline Officers' Association 104
Merchant Navy College 106
Merchant Navy Comforts Service 96, 104, 106, 112
Merchant Seamen's Office 10
Mills, Captain Michael 112
Ministry of Defence (Navy) 114
Ministry of Shipping 78
Missions to Seamen 55, 72, 74
Montanaro, Captain W. H. F. 75
Moray Outward Bound Sea School 98

Nadir Shah 4, 6
National Sea Training School/College 78, 104, 110, 112. 113
Nautical Institute 104, 108
Naval Club 22
Naval Education Service 112
Naval Lads' Brigade 89
Naval Officers' Widows' Fund 34, 104
Navy Board 44, 49
Navy League 89, 90, 96, 114
Navy League Boys' Naval Brigade 89
Navy League Sea Cadet Corps 89
Nelson, Captain (Admiral Lord) Horatio 22, 28, 41, 42, 49, 76
Nuffield, Lord 90

Oceana, tug 74
Officers' Association 104
Otway, Commander Robert 48
Outward Bound Movement 98

Palliser, Admiral Sir Hugh 34

Parker, Julian 104
Paul, William 66
Peninsular and Oriental Steam Navigation Company 76
Peters, George 10
Phillip & Son 112
Phipps, Captain 68
Plimsoll, Samuel 58-59
Pocock, Admiral Sir George 22
Port Jackson 72, 74-76, 96
Powlett, Captain Lord Harry; Duke of Bolton 19, 20
Premier, HMS 100
Prescott, John, MP 117
President III, HMS 80
Prince Louis 98
Protestant Britons of Norwich 22
Pyrgos 72

Queen Victoria Seamen's Rest 55

Racehorse 44
Ragged Schools 55
Raikes, Robert 8
Raikes, Thomas 8
Red Ensign Club 58, 71, 103, 104, 106
'Reformatories' 60, 62, 66, 80
'Refuges' 60
Resolute of Thames 110
Roberts, Captain Christopher 113
Romney, Earls of 14, 33, 68, 112
Royal Air Force 96
Royal Alfred, HMS 100
Royal Alfred Seafarers' Society 55
Royal Exchange 10, 24, 25
Royal Hospital School 20
Royal Mail Line 76
Royal National Lifeboat Institution 55, 108
Royal Naval Volunteer Reserve 62, 71, 80, 100
Royal Oak, HMS 96
Royal Trinity House Volunteer Artillery 49
Royalist, brig 110, 114
Russia Company 4, 6, 10, 22

Sadler, Whitchurch 67
Sailors' Home Trust 55, 56, 58, 70, 71, 78, 103, 106

Saunders, Sergeant Arthur 77
Sea Cadet Corps/Association 90, 96, 109, 113-114, 116
Seafarers' Education Service 92, 94-95, 98, 101, 102, 106, 108, 114
Sea Lines 108, 113
Sea Scouts 113
Sea Vision UK 117
Seamen's Hospital Society 55
Searcher, HMS 100
Seymour, Sir Michael 67
Shaftesbury, Earl of 21
Shaftesbury Society 60, 78
Shaw Savill & Albion Company 99
Shovell, Admiral Sir Cloudesley 14
Smith, Captain Graham 113
Smith, Richard or Robert 32
Snaefell, HMS 96
Society for Nautical Research 76
Society for Encouragement of Arts, Manufactories & Commerce 10, 22 (later known as the Royal Society of Arts)
Society for the Propagation of Christian Knowledge 26
Society of Antigallicans 22
Solebay, HMS 49, 50, 54, 56
Southampton, HMS 60
Spencer, Earl 22
St Barbe & Green 40
Star, Reverend Leonard 72
Stephens, John 21, 25
Stepney Society 20
Suckling, Maurice 20
Sunbeam, yacht 59
Sunday Schools 55
Synge, Archbishop Edward 26

The Seafarer (the Marine Society journal) 102
Thorn, HMS 44, 48, 49
Thornton, Cornwall & Company 14
Thornton, John 2, 8, 9, 10, 14, 33, 34, 38, 56 and *passim*
Thornton, Richard 110
Thornton, Samuel 38
Trincomalee, HMS 54, 109
Trinity Ballast Office 44
Trinity House 20, 22, 49, 104

T. W. Ward, shipbreakers 95
Tyrawley, Lord 2, 6

U-boats 76
Unicorn, HMS 54
United Nations Educational, Scientific & Cultural Organisation 92
University Extension Journal 90

Venedotian 92
Venus, HMS 54-55, 56, 59, 109
Victory, HMS 76
Villiers, Alan 98
Vindicatrix, HMS 78, 104
Victualling Board 37

Walker, Fowler 19
War Library Service 96
War Office 92
Ward, Captain G. P. 72, 74.
Warsash School of Navigation 110
Warspite
 I 59, 60, 62, 66;
 II 67, 68, 69, 71, 72, 75, 78;
 III 80, 81, 84, 87, 88, 89, 95, 98
Watson, Alderman Brook 38, 40
Watson, Lucy 14
Watts, Edmund 112
Wellesley, HMS 60
Wesleyan Seaman's Mission, (became Queen Victoria Seamen's Rest) 55
Westminster Fishmarket Trust 44
Wilberforce, Willliam 8, 55
William IV, HM King 36
Woodward, Reverend Doctor Josiah 26
Workers' Educational Association 90
World Association for Adult Education 92, 95

ACKNOWLEDGEMENTS

The publishers are grateful to the following for their permission to copy and reproduce illustrations for this book. All other illustrations are from The Marine Society collection.

Ambrose Greenway Collection: pp 95, 116; Authors Collection: p 77; James Ford Bell Library, University of Minnesota: p 7; Coram Family in the Care of The Foundling Museum: p 10; Rick Hogben Collection: p 74; Jan Kozak Collection, National Information Service for Earthquake Engineering, University of California, Berkeley: p 9; The House of Lords: Front cover, p 47; © Mary Evans Picture Library: p 13; © National Maritime Museum, London: pp 5, 27, 31, 43, 53; © National Portrait Gallery, London: pp 18, 21, 51; Parker Gallery: p 81; The Peabody Museum, Massachusetts, USA: p 1; Sothebys: p 83.

Every effort has been made to obtain permission for the reproduction of the illustrations in this book; apologies are offered to anyone whom it has not been possible to trace or contact.

© The Marine Society and Sea Cadets 2006

Published by The Marine Society and Sea Cadets, 202 Lambeth Road, London SE1 7JW.

All rights reserved. No part of this publication may be reproduced, stored in any retrieval system or transmitted in any form or by any means, electronic, mechanical, photocopying, recording or otherwise, without prior written permission of the copyright holder for which application should be addressed in the first instance to the publishers. No liability shall be attached to the author, the copyright holder or the publishers for loss or damage of any nature suffered as a result of reliance on the reproduction of any contents of this publication or any errors or omissions in its contents.

ISBN 0 9525292 2 X

Designed by Peter Dolton
Design, editorial and production in association with
Book Production Consultants plc, 25–27 High Street, Chesterton, Cambridge CB4 1ND, United Kingdom
Printed and bound in Singapore by Kyodo Printing Co (Singapore) Pte Ltd